DOGS

and a

COTTAGE

By the same author

Honorary Dog

DOGS

and a

COTTAGE

DORA WRIGHT

EDITED BY NAOMI PARKER

HiP

HISTORY INTO PRINT

First published in 2006 by Naomi Parker,
75 Whitstable Road, Canterbury CT2 8EA,
in association with History into Print,
Studley, Warwickshire, B80 7LG.

ISBN 1 85858 307 1

The moral right of the author has been asserted.

A catalogue record of this book is also available from the British Library

Typeset in Classical Garamond
Printed in Great Britain by
SupaPrint (Redditch) Limited,
Unit 19, Enfield Industrial Estate,
Redditch, Worcestershire, B97 6BY

Designed and typeset by News Broker Services,
48 Station Road, West Wickham, Kent BR4 0PR

Contents

In loving memory of Dora Wright
(1920-2001)

1
I Am In

It was dark when I awoke, and cold. I was sticky with sweat and waves of terror swept over me in the blackness, leaving me weak and shaking. And where was I? Groping for sense and orientation I began to remember. I was in the cottage. My cottage. I had actually managed to buy my cottage, the object of my desire for so many desperate months. I had moved in - just moved in, and should now be sleeping the blissful sleep of triumphant exhaustion, not lying shivering and trembling with sheer funk.

Orientation began to win over disorientation. This unfamiliar narrow bed was my spare bed. My lovely cosy double bed was even now lying in the wintry garden because it had proved too wide to go up the steep staircase, and I was freezing because the bedclothes had slid off me onto the floor.

And of course I wasn't alone. Deep breathing from my double box spring mattress, put down in the middle of the floor, reminded me that my bed's misfortune was a piece of good luck for my three dogs.

Sitting up, I hauled the recalcitrant blankets back into position and prepared to lie down again.

As I did so a wet cold nose was pushed into my ear and my face received an energetic licking. Sunshine, my senior Airedale, was doing her best both to give and receive happiness and reassurance.

Gladly I returned her caress with a hug and a kiss, lay down again and, comforted, went back to sleep. In this manner did one chapter of my life come to an end and another begin.

To be cast adrift on the world by the disintegration of a twenty-year marriage in one's early forties is unnerving enough.

To try to rebuild with one's slender resources and the partnership of friends only to have it all collapse again in bitterness and enmity ten years later is even worse. My first half-century was behind me when I spent that first night in my cottage, and that narrow bed in the inky downstairs room was only attained after nearly two years of war on all fronts.

I was drained of every resource I had: money, health, tenacity and courage. The waves of terror that woke me that night and every night for the next fortnight only served to remind me how near I had come to total disaster.

Did I say every resource? Not quite. I still had my dogs, and then, as always, they were my lifeline.

2
How I Found It

If I started at the bottom when I attained my cottage it was at any rate the bottom of a ladder, and punch drunk as I was, I was yet all eagerness to begin the climb. My mortgage would seem laughable by today's standards, but it was still rather more than I could comfortably afford.

I had no reserves and no rich relations, only a minuscule maintenance allowance from my ex-husband, the skill in my hands and the breeding potential of two Airedale bitches.

The maintenance was roughly equivalent to the mortgage, so all the dogs and I had to do was to keep ourselves and pay the bills. All.

People have often asked me how I found my cottage, they think it is so out of the way. Well, I think I may claim to have approached the problem with a modicum of intelligence. First of all I drew a ten-mile circle round my vets' surgery. An odd idea? Not if your dogs are the most important thing in your life. Vets are like garages and if you have found good ones it is as well to stick like glue.

Of this circle I preferred the north western section as being nearer to my training club and to many of my trimming customers. I called this having a good position on the map and it was the first item on a short list of necessities which I drew up.

How basic they were, the others being a country situation, important if you are going to keep and breed dogs – a large garden – access for a car – water and electricity – and reasonably good condition of roof, walls and drains. I was so desperate I believe I would have waived that last condition if necessary (and it nearly was). Fortunately the cottage just scraped through. My cottage certainly had the first two of these requirements. Access for a car was unsatisfactory, being round the back of the other cottages via an overgrown communal drive in primitive condition.

The cottage is built on a bank which is several feet above the level of the lane and bounded by a stone wall but I thought a bulldozer could cure this and booked one, although it seemed reluctant to start work. Fortunately there was ample room at the side for a sloping drive to be dug out and this was done just the day before I moved in.

Water turned out to be a bonus. It comes out of the tap like anybody else's, but the source is a spring which never falters even through the severest drought, and gives a sweet sparkling water better than any mains supply.

Drains also appeared to be like anybody else's. The difference was that they simply emptied into a stream in the bordering wood, that's all, and while this did bother me quite a bit I never forgot that but for this mediaeval feature I would probably never have had the chance to buy this dear little house at all.

It would have been snapped up by somebody else during the long miserable struggle which I waged to stake my claim to it.

Apart from this short list of necessities and the bonus of spring water my cottage has two other benefits.

It faces almost due south. I should probably still have bought it if it had faced north, but I love light, warmth and sunshine and this southerly aspect gives it always a warm and cheerful feeling.

The other bonus is a large shed at the bottom of the garden, large enough to allow me to put my puppy kennels under cover and allow ample playing room for my little ones even in wet weather. It was something I had always wanted. I just couldn't believe my luck.

When I first saw the house it was already under offer to a buyer who was having protracted problems in completing. For nearly eighteen months, while hunting for, rejecting or failing to buy other places, I badgered the agents about it. Every week I went into their office and asked was it sold?

It paid off and the day came when I was told the buyer had finally withdrawn and they were rewarding my persistence by offering it to me instead of advertising it. I remember how surprised the agent was when I gave him my cheque for the deposit and then asked for the keys so that I could look over it. He hadn't realised that I had never been inside!

He probably thought I was mad, but thanks to my short list I knew that this was the house for me and what I had glimpsed through the windows had been enough.

In fact when I did go inside I found that the last tenants had decorated it right through before leaving and all was clean and pleasant. Moreover the kitchen led into a conservatory which I could see would be perfect as a trimming room. Another bonus.

I had gone into my previous address with friends as a joint venture but it had all gone disastrously wrong. and before the end we were no longer friends but far otherwise. By the time I had finally regained the money I had sunk into it, acquired the cottage and moved in, I was in the state of collapse which I have described.

My slender capital had been spent in having the roof, gutters and some of the bedroom flooring repaired. My fiftieth birthday was behind me, it was March, it was cold and wet and I was very down indeed. But not down and out. I was down and in.

I could now close my own front door against the world.

3
Turning Point

It was strange how sharply my entry into the cottage marked the turning point in my fortunes. Up to that point everything went wrong and after it everything went well. My actual moving day proved a kind of crescendo. It was sheer hell from start to finish.

Always mindful of the safety of my dogs I had already seen to one essential item - garden fences.

A truly heroic octogenarian whose poodle I had trimmed for some years had nobly volunteered to take up my existing wire and posts so that I could transport them to my new house and get them erected before moving in.

For weeks he worked bare-armed in the cold to take down my fences, first shutting off the orchard, then the kennel section, eventually leaving only a small garden for my puzzled girls. As the rolls of sheep netting and the old hop poles were extracted I would load them into and onto my faithful minivan and ferry them the sixteen miles between the two places to dump them in the new garden.

A few days before the move my nephew, ably supported by his girl friend, kindly came over and helped me put them up again. As the new garden was a good bit smaller than the old one we were able to use the best material and jettison the rustier sections. I was also able to salvage enough old kennel gates to make temporary ones for my new establishment. So far so good.

I had also engaged a jobbing builder to do such repairs as seemed essential and booked a contractor to dig out a drive at the side of the house. All this, incidentally, while I was still not the owner of the property, but with the vendor's permission. What had he got to lose?

So the great day – March 12th, 1971 – dawned at last and began with the arrival of a man to cut off the telephone. Fortunately I felt this was too early and asked him if he would mind coming back later. As it transpired the day without the phone would have been absolutely impossible.

The next arrival was my dear daughter Naomi, complete with baby and always a tower of strength. Next the removal van and the first disaster. Its owner, engaged over the phone, had not bothered to view the job beforehand and instead of a pantechnicon, turned up with a vehicle about the size of a baker's van.

He took one look at the effects already stacked in the front garden, turned round and disappeared, to be seen no more. Armed with the yellow pages, I went to work on the phone but as expected, all removal firms were fully booked for the day. And I had to get out that day and no later.

At last a sympathetic voice offered the number of a friend who might be able to help as a private venture. Success. Yes, the friend would come although he was rising from a bed of 'flu to do so. He did – in a van not a lot bigger than the first one.

He also quailed when he saw the size of the job – I had kennels and other outside equipment to take as well as more ordinary household items – but being made of sterner stuff than his predecessor he asked permission to use the phone and called for help.

This resulted in the arrival of another like himself in a similar vehicle. Both these young men were accompanied by their wives and all four worked valiantly all day, ferrying stuff to the new address, unloading it into the garden to save time and then returning for more.

At last the end was in sight and I set off to the estate agents to collect the keys. Shock horror! They would not let me have them!

My erstwhile friends' solicitors refused to release the balance of my money until I was out! So there was I with my chattels spread between two addresses and no place to call home. I tore back with a sinking heart and confronted them.

They said they had to abide by their solicitor's dictum. Pointing out that we were equally anxious that I should quit their premises I suggested a compromise – we would finish emptying my rooms by turfing all my remaining effects into the garden. They could then inform the solicitors that I was indeed out, the money could be released and I could get the key and depart. This they grudgingly accepted and the key at last was mine.

Piling the dogs into the already overloaded Mini and followed by Naomi in her own car I at last arrived at my goal. The four tired helpers were already there and the garden piled like a shanty town with mysterious bundles. They helped us get the heavier and more perishable items inside and then I paid them, thanked them and told them to go, we would finish the rest.

The young man with 'flu didn't look too good but stoutly said he was all right. His wife however firmly insisted on putting him back to bed, so away they went. We never saw them again but remember them always with gratitude.

Thanks to the fences I was able to let the dogs into the garden, and as I had their dinners ready prepared I fed them. They then set out to explore, obviously very worried by all these strange proceedings.

In the cluttered and topsy-turvy house they were quite unable to settle down. We had found right at the start that my bed would not go upstairs. I can't say it worried me much as I knew by then that I could sleep standing up if necessary.

After the men had gone Naomi, who had worked like a Trojan all day, had to go too. She had over an hour's drive ahead of her, a baby to feed and put to bed and then dinner to prepare not only for herself but for her husband and some of his business colleagues. I think I had the easier prospect.

I couldn't find anything. Luckily there were strip lights in kitchen and sitting room but that was all, and the dogs were not helping.

Shaken to their souls by the day's upheavals and what must have seemed to them our quite inexplicable exodus from the only home they had ever known, they roamed moaning from place to place, falling over heaps of chattels, and flatly refusing all invitations to lie down on cushions, piles of clothing, books or saucepans.

Shakily I made up my spare bed in the nook under the stairs and had just decided to take to it, preferably for life, when a wonderful and unexpected thing happened.

I knew no one in the village, yet in the next hamlet lived an old customer who had moved there some months before and whom I continued to visit. She was laid low with influenza or (she told me later) she would have come to my aid early in the day.

As it was, and ill as she was, she still thought of me, and a knock on the door announced her emissary. She had sent her husband to see if all was well.

He bore a bunch of freesias, a *Welcome to Your New Home* card, a thermos of coffee, a packet of sandwiches and an offer of assistance. That knock on the door was a turning point.

From the misery of the previous two years of struggle and all the stubborn difficulties of that dreadful day when every possible thing had gone wrong, I had reached the nadir of my strength and resistance. But on the pinpoint of that knock all changed and everything began to go well.

He helped me drag the discarded mattress back into the sitting room, where it was at once thankfully slumped on by all three dogs, who were thereafter at peace.

He went home for matches, light bulbs, soap, a torch, all essentials still buried in the pile, and finally departed with my choking thanks and the snores of the dogs ringing in his ears.

I had done it, against all the odds I had done it!

I was camped out in a jumble of old, worn household goods and couldn't lay my hands on anything I wanted. I had electricity and water and that was about all. I was quite alone apart from the dogs, tired out and denied even the comfort of my own bed. But I was where I had struggled so hard to be, and from now on all things were possible.

4
We Begin

Waking on that first morning I looked round my ideal home and found it a picture of considerable disarray. I'm told that there are removal firms which not only transport your household goods but unpack and arrange them for you before leaving. It definitely hadn't been like that for me, but I wasn't complaining. I was in and that was all that really mattered.

The big mattress was the first thing that caught my eye now, and my woolly friends rose as one dog at the first sign that I was awake. They approved unanimously of having a box spring in the middle of the floor but were rather worried by the rest of the set-up.

It was up to me to reassure them by my own attitude, so I returned their anxious good-mornings with hearty hugs all round and got up to tackle the day.

The first job of any day at all is to let the dogs out, and thanks to my foresight in getting my fences erected before moving in I was able to do this with an easy mind. I had personally brought over every post and roll of wire from my last garden on my roof rack. It took a good few journeys as that garden had included half an acre of orchard, but fencing was too expensive an item to leave behind. The inside of the van on those trips had been occupied by batches of paving stones, also too useful and pricey to lose.

My new garden was a fifth of an acre, a lot smaller, but it would have to do and was really as much as I wanted to cope with single-handed. My three tore avidly up and down it, noses to ground in passionate curiosity while I turned my attention to the problem of breakfast.

My electric cooker was standing in the garden shrouded in polythene and I had no electric kettle. What I did have was a small and ancient Calor gas fire of the kind which hooked on to the front of a small cylinder. They used to be popular with roadmen, replacing the older but more picturesque brazier, and like a lot of simple but perfect things are no longer available.

This little fire had a flat openwork top and I had discovered that this would heat a kettle or saucepan quite nicely. By the time I had taken down the curtains (which were sketchily tacked up with drawing pins) the water was hot enough to make my morning coffee.

Breakfast over, it was a question of where to start. As far as I can remember my start was to find the electric drill and put up a curtain track and hang the curtains properly. This made me feel good as not only did I now have curtains that I could draw but once hung the curtains counted as something put away and no longer adding to the heap.

The kitchen was really the main problem as it had a very tatty cupboard running the length of the wall against which I wanted to position the cooker. This problem was soon solved by the same customer's heaven-sent husband reappearing, ripping it out and slinging it outside for me.

He asked me if I wanted the mattress out too, but the girls had reclaimed it and I was too weak-kneed to deprive them of such luxury in the midst of squalor.

The next arrival was the electricity man to put in the cooker, which he quickly did. The two kitchen cupboards which I had brought with me were now in place and vinyl on the floor, and while it wouldn't have looked out of place in Baron Hardup's castle, at least my kitchen was now a going concern. I began to feel encouraged.

The only good thing about my moving day had been that it was dry. I feel someone must have slipped up there. Most unaccountable, but whoever it was had realised their mistake and set about making amends over the weekend.

It now being Saturday I slipped out in the Mini to get a few weekend supplies, taking the girls with me in case they thought they were being deserted in this weird strange dump. But the lane is narrow and when I tried to turn back into my new drive I found that it had degenerated into a mud slide and no way was the car going to get back up it. My flounderings attracted the attention of my new neighbour, an inquisitive old countryman who lived in the adjoining cottage with his wife and unmarried son and was known to one and all as Tom.

On my visits to the cottage he had never failed to appear and displayed the liveliest interest in everything I did. Surfeited with neighbours as I was at the time I wasn't at all sure I was going to like this.

However, it looked as if Tom was going to be on my side, for he not only sympathised with me on the condition of the drive but told me to park the car at the Manor, two hundred yards up the lane.

I had bought my cottage from the Manor and Tom seemed to regard it as the most natural thing in the world that I should avail myself of its capacious sheds. As I couldn't leave the van stuck across the lane it seemed best to agree.

Tom helped me to slew it round and I drove off and parked with a heartening sensation of being less alone in the world than I had thought, especially as Tom's reaction to the girls had been one of respectful admiration and pleasure.

I had less luck in finding suitable rubble for the drive although this was an urgent priority, and when I did find some it was only enough to spread a thin layer over half of it.

However I did have a lot of paving stones so I used these to cover the upper part and these worked so well that they are still there, a little camouflaged now by encroaching grass but doing a perfectly adequate job.

5
First Summer

T he dogs who constituted my whole household in those days were named Sunshine, Socks and Sadie. The eldest was Sunny, then five years old. Sunny was a little thing as Airedales go, vivid in colour, joyful, gentle and lively. If ever a dog was well named it was Sunny for she loved everyone and was always happy and smiling.

Socks was the daughter of my best beloved Solo who was killed on the railway line when Socks was only two months old. Although it had happened nearly five years earlier, it is not too much to say that this tragedy contributed to my deplorable lowness on taking over my cottage, for I had not got over it then and haven't got over it now nor ever shall.

On the loss of her mother, Socks had transferred her allegiance to Sunny who was then herself only seven months old, and loved her dearly to the end of her life.

I would not have kept Socks had it not been for the loss of Solo, and I kept her as much for Sunny's sake as my own. She was a funny old thing, not like Solo in any respect at all. It was obvious from her earliest days that she was not going to be a good breed specimen.

She kept her ears obstinately folded and they stuck out sideways like wings. Her stifles were straight, her hind movement suspect, and to cap it all she proved to have a heart murmur.

I decided very early in Socks' life that she had better not be bred from, still I loved her for her own sake. She was all I had of Solo and I never regretted keeping her although a lifelong passenger was really not a thing I was well equipped to support at that stage.

Sadie was Sunny's daughter and had already had one litter when we moved. I had sold Sadie to friends when she was a baby but they only had her a few weeks when a change in their domestic circumstances made it impossible for them to keep her.

They gave her back to me and I decided she should stay. I already had her litter sister Star, but Star developed a faulty mouth, and as this is a very difficult fault to breed out, I felt that she would have to go as I certainly couldn't afford to keep two non-breeding passengers.

My son Stephen who was working for the Guide Dogs suggested that she could go there. He trained her himself and I am proud to say that she gave a long life of good service in this work.

You will notice that all my dogs' names begin with the letter S. This is something I started with Solo and have kept up ever since. The odd thing is how often their names have turned out to be very apt for them after they have grown up.

Socks was warm, woolly and a trifle comical, Sadie was a lady, a little prim and stand-offish, while Star as a Guide Dog was certainly the star of the family.

My current three soon settled down in their new home. Sunny took up the job of guarding the front fences and Socks the back ones. I find my dogs always make this arrangement, and on the death of one of them another 'unemployed' member will take over in her place. They also barked for the front door and howled for the phone - a useful habit if I was out of earshot of the bell.

Sadie's special talent was for opening doors. She had taught herself this at our previous home where the way to the garden was through the French window. She had become very expert, being able to cope with the lever handle whether coming in or going out without any scrabbling or untidy work, resting one paw on the fixed door frame while she manipulated the handle on the other in quite a dainty manner.

She found the cottage a challenge as we had several different types of door catches. She got the hang of the sliding door at once and the front door being opened by a lever handle presented no problems unless locked. The bedroom doors have old-fashioned latches which have to be lifted up on one side or pressed down on the other. These too she soon mastered. The sitting room door is held by a pretty stiff press button and I had to admire her technique with this one, which was to insert one claw in the crack and jerk it until it popped off the button, after which it could easily be opened by any casual paw.

Sadie got so good at this that if one of the other dogs wanted to go out I could simply ask Sadie to open the door. She would get up and do so and then quietly lie down again. However I did draw the line at her opening the garden gate and going for a stroll at will, and managed to fit a bit of plastic covered wire in such a way as to prevent the latch working.

A lot of Airedales have this door-opening knack and many people who have bought puppies from me have told me that no door is safe against them. But of those I have kept myself only Sadie has really developed this talent. I don't count the usual habit of pulling doors open: the ability to work a catch or handle is something else.

One of Sadie's grandsons indeed not only opened doors but was taught by his mistress to shut them as well. I found that visitors were slightly unnerved on seeing the door opened by a dog letting herself in or out. To have it close the door behind it as well must have made them wonder if they were seeing things.

Having had continual complaints about my dogs barking from my former co-tenants, I worried a good deal about them upsetting my new neighbours. There were four cottages in this row, built as two semi-detached pairs, but when I expressed anxiety on this point Tom stoutly denied that the girls were noisy.

'You expect them to bark when somebody goes by,' he said 'and with you living alone in the end house you want people to see you've got good dogs.'

I found out later that there had previously been a large dog chained in the garden of my cottage which had barked and howled non-stop. No wonder Tom thought my lot were quiet. He also told me that when I was out they rarely made a sound at all until three minutes before my return, when they would set up a howl, obviously having heard the approach of my car as I came through the village. Others have since verified this, to my great relief as it was definitely not what I had been told before.

I had thought the dogs would feel the loss of their much bigger garden and orchard, but it was soon obvious that they were every bit as happy with this new one and it wasn't difficult to understand why.

Our other situation had been very secluded, with nothing to be seen through the fences but a tangle of grass and bushes. But here it is very different, with interest on all sides.

The front fence is right over the lane where cars, tractors, people and horses may be seen. The fence adjoining this on the house side gives a grandstand view of the drive and front door where all callers can be inspected and rude words shouted at them.

The long side fence borders a wood where birds, mice and other small creatures live. The field at the back is the home of some horses, while the other side fence divides us from the next garden.

Here the girls usually found Tom, and he was always ready to talk to them, though I'm afraid they repaid him ungratefully by shouting their insults at his own two dogs.

Bimbo was very old and died fairly soon after our arrival, the other, a Labrador bitch named Slipper, was too nervous of our invasion to come to the fence but stood, a menacing black shape, immobile and growling on the far side of Tom's garden.

6

Pioneering

With so much to do I hardly knew where to start. Moving in March also meant that my busy Spring trimming season was just beginning. The money was more than welcome, but how precious my weekends became.

My new drive had been dug a little too close to the house and I was scared of subsidence, so one of my first jobs was to consolidate its steep sides by building walls to hold the soil.

I chose ragstone for this to match the existing front wall. There was quite a lot of it lying around as it is contained naturally in the ground here. I collected all I could find and got a good start on my walls. There were also a few pieces of natural paving stone, just enough to make a little flight of three steps from the side path down to the drive.

Long before I was finished my supply of stones ran out and I had to find more. Money to buy it was simply not there. In the little valley on the other side of the wood, however, an old orchard had just been grubbed out and I could see many tempting chunks of stone scattered on the rough ground.

I asked the farmer if I might collect some and permission was readily granted. I suspect I was doing a useful job there as so much random hard core did a lot of damage to the farm machinery.

So, taking a dog each time for company, I spent some pleasant afternoons collecting stones, loading them into the mini and then ferrying them home. As the summer went on, I got into the habit of going outside after breakfast and spending an hour building my walls before starting work.

My neighbour from the cottage at the other end of the row (who was also Tom's daughter-in-law) would stop on her way past with her baby girl and stand and laugh at me. There's nothing funny about seeing a man building a wall, but a woman? It's still a man's world, so I obligingly joined in the laugh and thus began a great friendship. Dot and all her family became so close to me that the hard edge of aloneness soon began to melt away and I felt almost as if I had a family of my own within call.

Strange to think that I came into my cottage with a neighbour phobia intense enough to repel all boarders and then found myself among neighbours so warm and friendly that only a pathological misanthrope could have resisted them.

To me in that first summer it was another dimension of the healing spell which my new home cast on my bruised spirit and indeed on all my affairs.

By the time the sun was strong in the heavens I had stopped licking my wounds and was getting stuck into my jobs with energy and enthusiasm.

Although I say it myself I have a definite talent for pioneering. I would have been a wow on a wagon train or on the construction side of building a log cabin, just so long as no one asked me to scrub the floors or keep the place dusted. My forte is creation rather than maintenance.

I spent many happy hours during the war and the subsequent lean years coaxing other peoples' cast-offs to live again as a pair of baggy rompers or minute tweed coat for my offspring, and many are the wire fridge shelves, part-worn hop poles and dismembered cupboards which have contributed to the building of my estate.

Why, the first garden gate I erected here was not only made from the best bits of several ex-kennel gates, but its centre panel was actually a survival from our air-raid shelter. As this was issued in 1941 I think that's quite good going. Although I afterwards installed wrought-iron gates, this steel mesh panel still survives, and only recently came in useful to plug a hole in the back fence caused by a tree falling on it.

It's a nice thought that all over Britain a grateful generation has used this gift of a benevolent government to keep its dogs, fowls and rabbits from straying.

I planned to mate both Sunny and Sadie at their next heats, so making provision for puppies was a top priority in that first summer. I already had a good whelping box and indoor puppy pen, a second box was lent by a breeder friend and another pen contrived from odds and ends.

The two small front rooms, one upstairs, would easily convert to maternity wards, but providing outdoor accommodation was a bigger problem.

I had the big shed at the top of the garden and two kennels to put inside it. These kennels were no longer in prime condition and I would not have considered them adequate in the open, but they were ideal to use under cover.

The main trouble was the shed floor, which was of earth. I gritted my teeth. No good blinking the problem, I was going to have to concrete it. The shed is fifteen feet square, and that's a lot of concrete.

This pioneer's method of mixing concrete is to do it in a wheelbarrow, stirring with a hoe as when making a cake. It was a long drag from the drive, where my materials were dumped, to the end of the garden and into the shed, so the necessary water made the journey by hose.

So with many a groan and over several weeks, I persisted in this way until half the floor was done, with a neat drain (gouged out with an old tennis ball) discharging under the wall into the garden. Phase One of the floor was complete.

It was surprising how many old battens and strips of timber I had brought with me. I was able to fit up the concreted part as an inside run with an easily movable partition cutting it in two without spending a penny on wood.

Wire netting (more old stock) completed the picture with a couple of light wire gates also constructed of battens and netting. To tell the truth it looked a bit Heath Robinson (like most of my pioneering efforts). However it has worked beautifully ever since.

I had long ago lined the insides of the two kennels with hardboard which I had painted white so that anyone could easily see that they were clean. In the dimness of the shed this also gave valuable reflected light, so I gave them another coat for luck. Now only one thing was needful. I hate to see dogs, and especially puppies, lying on concrete. I can feel the cold striking up through their little bones, so although my concrete was laid over a thick layer of plastic sacks for dryness, I determined to put down a wooden false floor.

But what to use? Even in those days a space fifteen feet by seven foot six was likely to be very expensive to cover with new wood. But here Naomi came to my rescue. Prefabs were being demolished near her Canterbury home and materials sold at (literally) knockdown prices.

For about seven pounds she was able to get me enough slabs of thick plywood to cover the floor of the inside pen. I happily sawed it to size, numbering the slabs so that I knew where they went as I intended to take them up between litters. They could be scrubbed and the concrete swilled down with disinfectant and left to dry until the next family moved into the shed.

There is quite a large space behind this big shed, about twenty feet by thirty, which makes an ideal outside run, warm, well drained and sheltered from the winds on all sides. With a little paving from gate to door and a makeshift fence I felt my puppies would be living in luxury, and so it proved.

While this, my kennel establishment, looks humble enough from the outside, inside it is really a warm and pleasant place to be. Puppies have plenty of scope and thrive happily there, my only reservations being that I can't see them from the house and that it is a long wet walk to deliver the late night feed.

7

The Sixteen

Part of the blight which had fallen on me and my fortunes in my previous home had been a dearth of puppies. There are some years during which no matter what you do, it seems impossible to get enough saleable puppies to cover your outgoings, which are always considerable.

I had never had two litters at the same time, but in our first cottage summer I mated both Sunny and Sadie and awaited the outcome with bated breath and permanently crossed fingers.

Everything seemed so right in our new home, would this all-important thing go right too? It did. The cottage magic worked and to my relief I had two pregnant Airedales on my hands and redoubled my efforts to be prepared for this dual event.

Sunny was first, and she went into the small downstairs room as she had become very heavy. Sadie, younger, taller and probably carrying fewer puppies, was better able to manage the stairs, so the spare bedroom was earmarked for her.

Sunny's first puppy ever had been Sadie's litter sister Star, the future Guide Dog. On that occasion I had sent for the vet as Sunny had been working really hard for nearly an hour without result. I never allow a bitch to strain for longer than an hour without yelling for help because the vet is unlikely to arrive in less than another half hour, and if he is tied up elsewhere it could be longer.

Anyway, why should the poor dog be allowed to exhaust herself when she probably still has hours of work ahead of her before the litter has all arrived?

You can easily lose puppies that way and may even lose your bitch. In this case help proved to be essential as not only did Star prove to be a big thick puppy, but she had her forelegs laid back along her chest, increasing her girth, and worst of all she was on her back so that the curve of her body went contrary to the natural curve of her mother's vaginal passage.

In short, Sunny could not possibly have expelled her unaided.

The vet however made short work of this problem and Star was soon delivered unharmed without even the aid of forceps or any other instrument than his hands.

It hurt poor little Sunny as she testified by a terrified yelp. All was then plain sailing and she produced another four pups making a litter of five. But she never forgot the occasion and the mere sight of that vet to the end of her days was enough to make her shake like a spindrier.

This time she had obviously decided that it wasn't worth all that trouble for a niggardly five pups. She produced eleven, all alive although some were very small, the tiniest, a bitch, weighing in at a meagre six ounces, half the usual weight.

Exhausted by giving birth to so many, Sunny was unable to produce the vast amount of milk that they required. This meant that I was going to have to keep them topped up, and out came the feeding bottles, the rubber teats, the warming saucepans, the packets of Casilan and glucose and all the paraphernalia inseparable from the job of 'supplementing'. It also meant that I would have to clean their rear ends, this being a job that many delicately nurtured Airedale ladies consider beneath them, including Sunny.

Four days later Sadie, with a minimum of fuss, produced two boys and three girls of her own in the little spare room at the top of the stairs. Sadie's children were always very big and every one of this five turned the scales at a pound and a quarter, more than three times the size of Sunny's little Mouse. Sadie's milk bar, moreover, was literally overflowing with best Gold Top. It was hardly surprising that the day after giving birth I found her crying outside Sunny's door. Obviously we both had the same idea.

So after getting her comfortable and sleepy in her own nest I took up the three smallest from Sunny's brood. She looked up with interest when I carefully put them in the furthest corner of her box and watched closely as they started to make their way across it towards that appetising smell of warm milk.

No growl as they began to burrow into the row of rightful heirs. I talked lovingly, approvingly, softly and constantly. Down came her nose. Out came her tongue, gently caressing. If only all adoptions could be as simple and safe as that.

The girls now had eight children each and there were three less to supplement, the bottle having instantly lost its appeal to the lucky pups now transplanted into the land of plenty.

How odd they looked. Although five days the senior, they nestled there like mice among a row of young hippos. It was then that Mouse got her name, because the view of her rump and little tail, which was all that could be seen of her, was exactly the same in shape and size as the rear end of a rubber mouse of the kind sold as playthings for pets.

So the litter upstairs presented no problems. The babies in the ground floor front, on the other hand, all needed a great deal of assistance. Luckily for me, Dot was intensely interested in the new arrivals, pedigree litters being a new experience for her. She was their first visitor and it wasn't long before she was helping with the tedious job of bottle feeding.

Hand feeding eight puppies is an interminable job and I was so thankful that Sadie had taken the other three. I fed Sunny's eight four times a day and it was heartening to see how much it brought them on.

A mixture of Casilan, glucose and cow's milk had been recommended to me by a friend who bred Lakelands and I also found the recipe in a book on breeding poodles. It gave really excellent results.

Although puppies obviously like the more costly products which imitate a bitch's milk, I not only found them to be almost prohibitively expensive but so thick that a weak puppy could not draw it from the rubber teat even with the feeding hole enlarged.

The Casilan mixture gave a sweet, very thin liquid which fed easily. Even then I always enlarged the teat holes with a red hot darning needle to the point where the milk would dribble from it if the bottle was held upside down.

Hungry pups love a bottle and the relief to the worried Mum must be considerable. I took pride in my bitches leaving their litters in 'good nick'. They would drop nearly all of their hair at the end of weaning, but their next coats would be extra good. They never had ribs sticking through their skin, and they were lively and full of fun.

The secret of bottle feeding is to keep the tail of the bottle well up so that there is no air in the teat. If there is, the pup will swallow that as well as the milk and not only will it blow up with wind but it will not have room for all the food it might otherwise take.

You often see 'personalities' on television take the feeding bottle from the keeper to feed some infant animal which is in the news. They hardly ever keep the tail of the bottle up enough and there am I jumping up and down in my chair and yelling 'Keep it up! Keep it up !' They never take any notice of me.

Dot soon got the hang of things and even Christina lent a hand. Young as she was – two – she was completely bowled over by the puppies and, so long as I was there, Sunny was quite happy to let her stroke and watch them.

Airedale bitches in my experience are always willing to co-operate when their attendant humans wish to handle their offspring and this is a great help in the management of a litter.

Not all breeds are so compliant. A friend of mine who kept another – I won't name it – often lost puppies because the mother would not let her get near enough to render necessary assistance.

During the birth of a litter, it was my practice to lift the newborn whelps out of the box while their dam was busy producing the next, and to pop them onto a hot water bottle in the 'cradle' – a small wooden tomato skip – laying a newspaper over the top to keep their warmth in.

This cut out the risk of accidental damage and they could quickly be put back as soon as things quietened down again.

A bitch can do quite a lot of damage stamping about and scratching up bedding during parturition but usually has periods of rest and quiet in between arrivals when she will be glad to have her babies around her.

Scooping ten infants back into the skip and wondering when Sunny was going to stop shucking out little Airedales, I noticed the headline on the covering news sheet. It read STAND UP AND BE COUNTED. Glassy eyed as I was by this time, this tickled my sense of humour.

I kept the paper, and, after Sadie's puppies had brought the count to sixteen, I put the whole bunch into the skip – they tended to overflow a bit – and got Dot to hold them up to the window with the headline behind them while I took their photograph.

A litter always means hard work and two litters seemed to more than double that. They arrived in September, which meant that all this hard labour coincided with the Autumn trimming rush which is second only to the Spring one. Under these circumstances there was only one way to tackle the situation and that was to put all other ideas out of my head except work.

I rose at six to plough through the day's opening chores in time to reach my customers early and get home again in good time for the next feed. Weaning was a maddening time, puppies having to be fed one or at most two at a time, and kicking up a great fuss at the mere idea of eating from a bowl.

I think I can claim to have got it down to a fine art, but oh, the relief when they at last reached the stage of wolfing everything put down, and all eating it together.

However that day did come at last, and at the age of five weeks they were able to move up into the big kennel. They went as a single litter – Sadie's lot were still so butch in comparison with Sunny's that there was never the slightest risk of confusing them, and their two mothers were quite happy with this arrangement. And any pup could latch on to either bitch and it would be fed and kissed whether it was her own child or not.

Socks too was thrilled with all these young ones and obviously enjoyed looking after them, while their own parents accepted her help completely without jealousy or resentment. It was a very happy, if exhausting, time.

Having the puppies living at the top of the garden had a lot of advantages but it meant a lot of running up and down for me. The feed I really dreaded was that late night supper.

By the time it was due, I was woozy with sleep after my strenuous day. Preparing the meal was bad enough, but taking it up to them in the dark was sheer hell.

Having no electricity in the shed, I had to carry a torch as well as the food and the dishes. The grass was usually wet, the trees too if it had been raining, and I had to wear boots and mac for the trip – often put on over pyjamas.

A struggle with the gate, a struggle with the big heavy door, then down with the dishes and pour out the supper – usually rice pudding with extra milk – before opening the inner gate and letting the sixteen out.

But it did my heart good to see how my efforts were appreciated as sixteen little snouts dived into the dishes and everybody put in some really strenuous lapping. Then most of them would trot out into the dark run to be clean while I collected the dishes and did my best to pick up the patches of soiled sawdust by torchlight while waiting for them to come in.

It was always warm and cosy in the shed, whatever the weather, and I felt my brood were well provided for.

It wasn't easy to count all sixteen in the dark. Sometimes the number would be short and I would have to send my torch beam probing the corners of the run to find some anti-social pup who had decided to sleep in the long grass instead of coming in to the cosy kennel, but at last the inside gate would close on them all. I never insisted on their going into the inner kennel, but left its door ajar with a sack hanging over the opening. Usually they went in, and this system allowed them to come out if they needed at night and avoided them soiling their bedding.

Shut the big door. Shut the pen gate. Down the long path to the house, not forgetting bucket, dishes or torch, the journey made easier in this direction by dim light from the house.

By the time I got in, locked up, shed my outer garments and washed up all the puppy gear, at least three quarters of an hour would have gone by. I would be shivering and very often wide awake as well.

When my two litters were six weeks old, I rang the local paper and asked if they were interested in sixteen puppies. They were, and the following week a picture appeared of the whole lot erupting from a huge dog basket.

It had taken Dot and me a lively quarter of an hour to get them all in it at once. The press picture resulted in at least one sale. Other customers came in answer to advertisements or through recommendation, and some were already waiting. Before long all sixteen had gone.

8

Digging In

Having lived in my cottage for thirty years, it is hard to look back and remember just when various jobs were done or even in what order. The seventies shot by like some strenuous dream, trimming punctuated by welcome but hard working weekends.

Summer was always my time for major improvements as I have more energy when it is hot. Cold weather, especially if wet or windy, reduces me to a shivering heap longing for the fireside.

Eliza Dolittle was right when she yearned for that room with its enormous chair and coal fire: we're obviously twin souls. But summer, lovely summer, is a different world altogether, and not one passed by without my achieving at least one improvement to my establishment.

Since nearly all my jobs are done by my own two hands, that establishment became more and more unique – or shall we say personalised - every year.

Unable to afford professional workmen, I felt it was much better to have a go myself than to sulk. This philosophy had the advantage that if met with only imperfect results, at least there was no one to reproach me with my failures. And it was fun.

Working out how some task never before attempted might be done gave me a lot of pleasure and an eagerness to get at it which was invaluable, because it is when I feel that way that I do my best work.

Naomi is the same. She is the best interior decorator I know, and between us we have created an infallible rule – 'Never waste a valuable urge'.

Whether it's dressmaking, concreting, or anything else, our work will never be at its best unless we are champing at the bit to get on with it. When we are, when the urge is upon us, the job will be done better, more quickly, and more easily, and we shall enjoy doing it. Very much.

There is nothing splendid, picturesque or pretentious about my cottage. It is a simple little shack built on the same plan as a shoe box, with a plain sloping roof laid on top. Originally it was just that, a brick box backing up against its neighbour, with two bedrooms upstairs directly above two rooms downstairs and a staircase going up between them.

The front door is at the side so that the whole house is just twelve feet deep and the 'hall', wedged between front door and stairs, is rather less than one yard square. Both pairs of cottages were built to accommodate labourers working on the surrounding farm.

The date set into the front gable is 1861. At a later date some madly spendthrift landowner decided that something else was needed and built on the lean-to extensions that now give the pair kitchens and bathrooms. Not that they were designed as bathrooms then, of course – more likely coal holes and outside toilets – but these had been knocked into one and converted in a primitive fashion before my arrival on the scene.

This was lucky for me, as at the time of my Herculean struggle to buy, the dictum was 'No bathroom, no mortgage'. I was therefore able to claim that the house boasted a bathroom and fortunately no one examined it too closely.

The floors of these two extra rooms were concrete throughout, so there should at least have been no danger of mice in the kitchen. Nevertheless my evenings were constantly enlivened by scratchings and scurryings in these two rooms. The dogs would rush through screeching in mad pursuit and knock their heads in corners, under sinks and behind cupboards in their attempt to catch the creatures responsible. I got very tired of this, especially as they never caught anything.

One happy consequence of this building plan, if it can be called that, is that there is no water in the original house and no tank in the roof. I shall never, thank goodness, be awakened by icy floods from a cistern bursting above my head. The water is heated by a back boiler behind the living room fire. The pipes from this run through a cupboard built into an alcove which serves as an airing cupboard.

One day not long after my arrival, a movement in the hearth caught my eye, and there among the cinders was a mouse, presumably from the cupboard. I'm not particularly scared of mice but shouted for the dogs who were in the garden. My call was answered by Socks.

'Look at that!' I said, and pointed at the mouse, which was now frozen in fear. To my astonishment she seized him swiftly and accurately in one incredible movement, ran outside and disposed of him. He was never seen again.

Closer examination of my cupboard revealed a mousehole just above the floorboards. Advice was asked from the builder then repairing the bedroom floor, but his reply was a contemptuous 'No good stopping a mousehole, they'll only come back. You'll never get rid of them once they're in the floor.' Oh won't I, I thought, and laid a hefty concrete kerb in the cupboard where floor and wall met.

This kerb was six inches high and six inches thick and the entrance to the hole was first stopped with a large pebble. There's never been a mouse in that cupboard since, but the nightly scurryings and mad rushes into the kitchen continued.

The philanthropic landowner had not allowed his heart to rule his head to the extent of making a good job of his cottage extensions. One-brick thickness was cheaper than a wall nine inches thick, so naturally was used throughout.

And whoever heard of farm labourers needing damp courses when these were luxuries not often found even in the homes of their masters? The house itself was blessedly dry and warm, but the later additions were certainly not. At that date the back wall of the bathroom seemed as porous as blotting paper and was often saturated.

The previous tenant had made a brave stab at making these two rooms habitable by spraying the walls and ceiling thickly with a ghastly rubberised paint, electric blue in the kitchen and bilious orange in the bathroom, topped up with navy and white spots over both. Damp had encouraged subsequent leprous patches of mould, yet the paint was impossible to remove.

The only thing to be done was to cover it up. I hastily papered over the lot and put up polystyrene ceiling tiles in the bathroom. This gave me about twelve months before the paper began to slide quietly from the walls.

The overflow pipes from the hot water tank and the lavatory cistern both discharged down the back wall. They seldom seemed to stop leaking despite the attentions of several plumbers. Small wonder that this wall was permanently sodden.

I promised myself that one day I would make a real job of renovating that bathroom but in those early years there was really too much other work and not enough money, so I put it out of my mind and turned my attention to other things.

One of these was the amount of mud and other debris brought indoors by twelve busy feet. No one who has not lived with a number of dogs given full-time free access to both house and garden can have any idea of the dirt problem this can cause.

Sunny was a particular offender because she had taken over patrolling the front fences, and being very much on the qui vive, she was shooting out to repel boarders a hundred times a day. Her feet soon wore a deep groove along the fence and she would trot back panting blissfully and mired well above the pasterns.

I began hunting for anything vaguely resembling paving stones. Old bricks, quarry tiles, broken concrete and cobbles were soon arranged and cemented into a terrace inside the fence where the dogs had their favourite stamping ground. This looked very pleasant and not only greatly reduced the dirt problem but kept their claws short between trims.

In my second summer I also completed Phase Two of concreting the floor of the big shed, and laid some paving stones over the busiest part of the puppy run. One problem here was the way the shed was cuddled into the hillside, because heavy rain from Tom's garden was apt to run off into mine under the shed walls and lie inside on the floor.

Concreting the floor inside had raised it a few inches but was not a complete cure. It needed a drain gulley outside the shed wall. This was difficult as the space between the shed and Tom's fence was both narrow and sloping. With my bulk, clumsiness, palpitations and general ineptitude I was also going to have trouble getting down to gutter level. However.

First I concreted a ledge just a little lower than Tom's garden. When it was hard I could just about walk along it. From this vantage point I somehow managed to cover the sharp down slope with concrete rather as one ices the side of a cake to make a smooth wall. This just left the gutter at the bottom to do.

I was in real difficulty here. Wet cement is heavy stuff to heave about and I just couldn't reach into the gulley to do the job properly. This was one of those times when it is an advantage to be a roaring amateur unhampered by knowledge of correct procedures. Like a caged lion I prowled about my domain looking for ideas, inspiration, materials – and as so often happens, there they were.

The builder who had put up my new house gutters had thrown the old ones into the garden. It occurred to me that, being gutters, they were naturally gutter-shaped. Exceptionally heavy rain had also made my sand pile more than ordinarily damp. With a sigh of relief I made the connection and fetched the wheelbarrow.

I mixed a barrowful of sand and cement. Pushing it to the scene of operations – this alone was easier since I had added no water – I collected my small garden spade. From the corner of the shed I could just manage to throw spadefuls of mix along the gulley, and then brush the wall down and level the mix with a hoe. I repeated the operation from the other end and in triumph saw my mucky gulley now lined from end to end with the sandy mixture. All that now remained to do was to fetch sufficient lengths of old guttering, drop them end to end along the bottom and tap them gently into place.

It was a whole week before I dared to go back for a look, but hey presto! It had all set rock solid, every bit as well as if the concrete had been mixed and laid in the conventional manner. This dry cement trick has since been shown on television, but this was years earlier and certainly no one had told me about it. The drain is still difficult to clean and keep clear of weeds but it functions perfectly and the shed floor stays dry.

I certainly wore my mason's hat a lot in those early years, but there are few jobs more satisfying because they rarely have to be done twice. My chief difficulty was in obtaining materials as stone is very expensive and so heavy that even a ton of it makes a very small pile and doesn't go far.

9

Breaks

Was life really all work in those early years? No, there were even times when I actually got away, usually taking all the dogs with me, but sometimes leaving them at home with Dot. She proved to be a kind of special dispensation of Providence to me in those days. For the only time in my life I knew what it was to have help generously given when needed.

It was Dot who insulated my loft for me. At that time the trapdoor over the landing was so small that to me it looked impossible for anyone to get through it. Luckily Dot was as slim as a beanpole, brave and energetic. When she got up there she reported 'a lot of hay', which proved to be a huge nest built by many generations of house sparrows. It must have been a considerable fire hazard.

I passed plastic sacks up to her, she stuffed them with the nest material and passed them down again. Between us we took out nine sacks full, and only then was I able to send up the insulating material which Dot laid down between the joists. Those joists need to be seen to be believed, by the way. They are made of long unplaned branches, possibly of elm, and are squared off only on the underside where they meet and support the ceilings. With daylight clearly visible between the bricks of the gable ends you really knew it was a country cottage up in that loft.

My mother was then living with my brother and his wife in Bristol, and it was when I visited her that it was impractical for the dogs to come with me. However these visits never meant more than two nights away from home and Dot would not hear of me kennelling them.

There is no doubt they were happier at home, the back door open as usual to give them access to their garden. Dot, an early riser, would let them out soon after six, come and sit with them whenever she could, light a fire if it was cold, switch on the television, draw the curtains, shut them in at dusk and come round last thing at night to let them out for their last tinkles.

I always left all their meals weighed out and bagged up, with name labels included, tied in groups for each day and put in the fridge. Dot would get them out in the morning to defrost ready for feeding later in the day. In this way she did not have the job of weighing out every dog's meal.

Under these circumstances and given that they all loved her, you'd think they wouldn't have missed me. But one afternoon when I had left early for Bristol to come back the following day, the weather suddenly produced a cloudburst. Dot remembered that my bedroom window was wide open and ran round to close it.

But Socks, who like the others had always welcomed her, refused to let her go upstairs. She got ahead, turned to face her and stood with teeth bared and snarling. Dot decided the window would have to stay open and retreated, when Socks immediately reverted to her usual bumbling old self.

When I heard of this incident I was chiefly struck by the fact that Socks obviously knew I wasn't coming home that night and was taking the responsibility to be on guard in my absence. Dot was equally impressed.

Two days later she came round with two hundred pounds in notes, holiday money which she and Nobby had been saving, and asked me to put it up in my bedroom as she thought it would be safer there than in her own house!

There were two places where all the dogs could accompany me, my son's house and that of friends in Yorkshire who had bought an Airedale from me some years earlier. Both of these necessitated long journeys, especially as Stephen at one time lived in Scotland.

It was easiest as well as cheapest to go by road, and I once drove all the way to Scotland and back with myself, five Airedales, my luggage, their luggage and a case of tinned dog meat packed neatly into the minivan. The case was first put down on the floor in front of the passenger seat, and the softer holdalls with my luggage arranged as flat as possible on top of it. Odds and ends such as cameras, road maps, money and dog towels went into the door pouches and any other crevices. This left the passenger seat free for one of the dogs to ride on in comfort.

The floor of the van at the rear I always kept well lined with bits of old carpet, and the other four dogs would lie, like a row of sardines, side by side with their heads towards the front of the car. This actually left some empty space by the rear doors.

They were very well behaved on the road. Sunny was the only one who was ever a nuisance and she was in a way easier to take on a long distance than a short one. For the first ten minutes she would be on tip-toe, watching eagerly through all the windows and screaming dementedly at any animal we passed. In fact I've known her to shriek at nothing more exciting than a falling leaf.

I found the best thing was to keep her lead on, station her right behind me with the lead tightly drawn under my arm and held in one hand. In this way I was able to check her worst excesses until she settled down, which she usually did quite soon, and she would thereafter be no problem at all until we were nearly at our destination.

Long journey or short, familiar route or unknown, she always knew when we were on the point of arrival and go into her routine again. No one who has lived with dogs will be surprised at this. A dog's telepathic powers cannot be denied.

They did surprise me however on their second trip to Yorkshire. It had been two years since they had been there and we had many hours of travel behind us when we eventually rounded the corner into the lane leading to my friends' house two miles away.

As the van turned they rose as one dog, wagging, laughing and yipping with excitement. How on earth did they know? They hadn't even been looking out of the windows. Telepathy again? But this wasn't just an end-of-the-journey reaction, it was definitely recognition, and as far as I can remember my mind was too soggy with driving to be sending out any signals at all.

The worst road in the world to drive on to my mind is the M1. To tackle it in a small car is to enter a sort of motoring hell. I soon began finding ways to go north without soiling my tyres with its surface. The first time I tried the A1 as an alternative I had a delightful drive. The only problem was where to get the girls out for what the Americans call a 'comfort stop'. There were no service stations here as there were on the motorway.

I pulled off on a lay-by bordered with a suitably grassy margin and faced the task of getting my maniacs out safely. My dogs are trained not to leave the car by the side doors, so those can be opened to allow me to disembark, but the back doors are their road to freedom and when these are opened the whole bunch is liable to erupt like a volcano.

Sitting in my seat with all doors firmly closed I put all five on their leads and slipped four loops over the hand brake, then got out, extracted the one loose dog and took her for her ritual visit to the grass.

Back at the van I put her in at the driver's door, freed the top loop from the brake, lifted the remaining three, dropped the returning dog's lead over it and replaced the other three on top.

At the back door again I once more got out the next loose dog and repeated the whole process again and again and again until all five were comfortable to continue their long ride. It was a lot of trouble but I was determined not to have a bloodbath on the A1. Better to have the van awash than risk that.

I can't begin to describe how wonderful it was at the end of these visits to reload my mini and turn its nose once more towards Kent in the knowledge that my cottage, my very own cottage, was waiting for me.

The closer to home I got, the more anxious I became, until by the time we turned into the home lane I could hardly bear to look for fear that it had burnt down, been struck by lightning, or was revealed to have been just a figment of my imagination all this time and simply not there.

Once I broke down on the M1 just after leaving Toddington service station. I noticed sinister wisps rising from the bonnet and pulled on to the hard shoulder. I lifted the bonnet and somehow managed to remove the water tank cap without blowing my fingers off.

The resulting clouds of steam were so horrendous that another motorist actually stopped to see if I was all right. There really wasn't anything he could do but he promised to ring the RAC for me and I didn't have to wait much more than an hour and a half for help to arrive. A hose had gone and the radiator was dry.

The RAC man filled the tank and gave me a gallon of water for my jerrican and said I could get home if I kept my speed down to forty miles an hour and topped up the tank every thirty miles.

He was over-optimistic. I had to keep below twenty eight and refill at every tenth mile. Not so bad on the motorway but it's not at all easy to find places where you can get water in North London on a Sunday evening. It took me hours and hours to get home but we did eventually make it.

The car had to have a new engine afterwards so I suppose we were really lucky. I can't think how I would have got back with three Airedales not to mention all our impedimenta if the car had simply died on the way as it easily might have done.

The first time I went to Yorkshire we took the M1. It began to rain as we slipped out of my drive and by the time we reached the motorway it was a deluge. I had a snack at the first service station to give it a chance to stop. It didn't so I thought I might as well go on and drive out of it.

The downpour followed me all the way. I had my headlights on all day and had to keep below forty as well, because surface water and spray made it practically impossible to see and in my low-slung mini it was like driving through a swimming bath. Worse still, I could not see the signs and missed my exit. Splashing around in this dark, fluid and unknown country, the journey took me an incredible ten hours.

When I arrived, battered, bewildered and disorientated, my hosts commiserated with me on arriving in such a heavy shower when it had been so beautiful all day! No wonder I hate the M1. I'm sure it hates me and I never feel safe on it.

10

Busy Days

Despite my determination to avert my eyes from the dilapidation of my bathroom it was becoming more and more difficult to ignore, and the most humiliating point of any week was when a caller asked permission to use it. I had to be careful not to refer to it as the bog: it was too apposite.

Wallpaper hung in folds from the rear wall and the black vinyl floor tiles were all curling up at the edges. I bought a cheap piece of brightly coloured carpet to put down over them. This looked more cheerful, but what was going on underneath? Nobody lingered in my loo.

It occurred to me that something might be done to help by drying out the wall from outside. My bathroom backs onto a small yard, enclosed at that time by a disintegrating wooden fence. This fence kept out both wind and sunshine. Two overflow pipes discharged water which ran continually down the wall making a dark green swamp in which thistles and nettles grew more than six feet high.

I decided to clear this jungle and replace the fence with a really posh stone wall. This raised once more the problem of getting in large quantities of stone. It was going to be a big task and an expensive one, so I decided to make it that summer's main job.

First I cut down the vegetation with a riphook and raked out the underlying rubbish. Then I treated the roots with weedkiller, barring off the area from the dogs for a time until it was safe.

Still the overflows ran, covering the red brick wall with white powdery mould. Since I couldn't stop them, I thought it would it made better sense to guide the water into the drains and I did this by attaching lengths of hose to the pipes. It was typical of my whole estate that even these pieces of hosepipe had a history. I had been advised to keep a hose permanently laid from the house to the puppy shed in case of fire. I duly did this, but there's more to running a kennel than good ideas. Storm's daughter Saffron was a pup that year and I found her one day playing with a floppy black toy – a piece of hose. Puzzled, I looked around to find the garden strewn with hose of varying lengths from one to eight feet. She must have had fun chopping up my fire-fighting apparatus. I bought another hose but kept it coiled up and out of reach for safety's sake.

Anyway the yard was now a drier, lighter and more pleasant place in which to work. The next step was to demolish the fence, a simple job. Getting rid of it was more difficult, because the dogs were passionately interested and eager to help.

I had erected a temporary fence around the yard to prevent a mass breakout and now had to hurl shattered planks and worm-eaten posts over it into the garden more or less at random. When it was all out, I collected it into a pile beneath the birch tree to await proper disposal.

I've made some mistakes in my time but this one comes high on the list. No sooner was the old wood dumped under the tree than my pack of clowns was convinced there must be something buried underneath it.

Even after the old wood was removed and burned they continued to dig. Years later they are still digging. The Hole, as it came to be known, developed into their favourite garden feature. I try to be tolerant, but I must confess to some irritation when their tunnels run under the M1 or the patio suddenly caves in.

I took two weeks of holiday from trimming and every day drove to the local quarry to load up with chunks of creamy ragstone. Christina and sometimes her little brother William came with me and helped in the work.

A load covered the floor of the van evenly with a single layer of stone. I then had to drive onto the weighbridge, and it was wonderful how close we came to my five hundredweight target every time. I enjoyed these trips and so did the kids for my odd pursuits provided them with unending entertainment. The quarryman enjoyed our visits too, for he was fascinated by my two small companions. These blonde infants were not only angelically beautiful at that age but were so much alike that they were really something to see.

At the end of the fortnight I had a satisfactory pile of rocks and began work on the wall. The first walls I ever built were thin because my materials had been scanty, and one of my neighbours had predicted that they would soon fall down. They haven't done so yet but there's still time. This I was determined should be sturdier. It is a right angle with arms a foot thick, and the only wall in my entire property to boast a damp course.

I can see the funny side of this but since it butts onto that infamous back wall it seemed only sense to make sure it couldn't add to the problem.

So the wall was finished and is certainly an asset, but was the bathroom any drier? Well, no. The pieces of hosepipe had to be removed in winter, as they froze solid with the result that the overflows cascaded inside the bathroom instead of outside. I laid the pieces on top of the coal bunker for use the following summer, but by spring they had disappeared.

Saffron again, I expect – anyway, I never found them again.

11

Rat Wars

I have perforce developed a very efficient technique for coping with my inadequacies as a one-woman work force. I simply ignore the problems awaiting my attention. Unfortunately, although theoretically aware that my black spots are still there, I don't actually see them any more. This does have its advantages for my peace of mind and low-worry index but it does unhappily have the drawback that other people still see these domestic blots – and probably see them more clearly than I, blinded by habit, ever could.

The nightly scurry scurry, skitter skitter in the kitchen, followed by the mad rush and crash of pursuing dogs – how could I have ignored all this for so long? And the long slow disintegration of my combined bathroom and loo – how could I have borne it? In extenuation I can only plead that I knew perfectly well that rehabilitation of my bathroom was going to be an epic effort which would demand the concentration of all my mind and all my other resources too once it was begun.

So what triggered the necessary impulse? I hardly like to reveal it, but well – here goes. At this time there was a slight but constant drip from the waste pipe below the wash basin. I put down a small plastic tub behind the pedestal to catch it, and this tub I kept finding overturned. I blamed Spice the puppy for it as I had seen her pottering about in that area. But one evening, having set it right and then shut the door I found it overturned again in less than half an hour.

I also found in the bath one morning a small cigar-shaped object about half an inch long. Picking it out with a bit of tissue, I examined it in puzzlement. I knew what it looked like but couldn't believe it. I cleaned the bath. Next day there were no fewer than three similar objects there. They must be bits of garden debris dropped from the inquisitive whiskers of a dog, I told myself. Or perhaps sent flying by the shake of a rough hairy head. Still I could not or would not believe. Then one evening when I was getting coal from the bunker outside, a movement caught my eye and I saw a lithe shadow run deftly up the inner framework of the conservatory and vanish under the bathroom eaves. I could shut my eyes no longer. I had rats in the bathroom.

Moreover since it opens off the kitchen and the door sports a picturesque rathole probably left over from the last century, I had rats in the kitchen too and those evening scurries and rushes had been for rats, not mice.

Shame and an ingrained habit of doing things for myself led me to take what action I could. First I examined the conservatory and found that there was indeed a hole under the eaves. Then I borrowed a rat trap from Dot's husband Nobby. It was rather a rickety affair, a large wire cage with a tunnel entry and central platform for bait, but in fact it was only a day or two before I had my first rat, a young female.

Elated, I rushed round for Nobby, who shot it while it was still in the cage and kindly disposed of the corpse afterwards.

I washed the trap and reset it, but now I came up against the brains and resourcefulness of Rats United. The wires were rather bent at one end of the cage and the grateful noshers of my tasty baits found it convenient to get out that way after enjoying a good snack.

Wedging the trap firmly against a board to close the weak spot only held them for a day or two during which the bait was untouched. I tried goodies of all kinds, not just cheese (a thing I seldom eat and which I was buying solely for the rats) but crispy bacon rinds and even sultanas.

The dogs just couldn't understand why I was wasting these delicious titbits in this irresponsible way.

After a couple of days the food began to be taken again, but still there was no prisoner and I had to face the fact that the little beasts had simply learnt their way both in and out of the trap and were feasting at their ease.

I was obviously going to have no luck catching my enemies in the conservatory, I must tackle them in the house.

Returning the trap and being greeted with a chuckle and a reassuring - 'They're cunning little devils, they are. 'Tain't easy to fool a rat, mate!' – I put my mind to the campaign.

No one likes to use poison where there are domestic animals, so instead I bought a couple of spring-loaded rat traps like overgrown mousetraps. One was baited and put in the bath. It was never touched and there were no further droppings in there either. In fact I became convinced that Mr. Rat has a very good control over his bodily functions and doesn't leave calling cards if he doesn't wish you to know he's been around.

I put a trap behind the pedestal. No takers. I was beginning to have a real respect for the intelligence of these determined invaders.

Their high road ran from the hole in the conservatory into the bathroom roof, where they met the top of the hot water tank. This sits in a cupboard over the bath taps and protrudes through the ceiling a few inches, closed in by a neat hardboard cover. Once in the cupboard, they jumped out of a hole in the bottom into the bath.

No self-respecting rat was ever held up more than five minutes by hardboard, and, judging by the state of the cupboard floor and the aforementioned hole in the door, I imagine the tribe had been using this route for a long time. Possibly they had an entry through the roof for years before the plumbing was done, and the plumber may well have believed that he was keeping them out.

Reluctantly I decided I must use poison and put some in the cupboard in a deep tin lid. Some of it seemed to get spilt – perhaps an athletic rodent, leaping in the dark from the top of the cylinder, had landed in it – but none of it was eaten.

In all this time I had never been aware of my enemies attacking my own food. This was probably because I keep everything pretty well covered against flies and dust, and this protection usually took the form of tins or glass jars. Bulk stores of dog biscuits and biscuit meal lived in large plastic bins in the conservatory and on occasion I had found teeth marks on the edges of some of the lids, but nothing more. I had at this time a large kitchen cabinet which had an inbuilt bread compartment about half way up. I used to wrap my loaves in plastic for freshness and keep them in here.

At the time when I began to try poison, I had a definite feeling that the rats, knowing they had been spotted, were now fighting with the gloves off. They began to be more careless about leaving their calling cards – in all the scurrying and skittering years I had never seen an actual rat – and several times I found traces of gnawing on potatoes in the vegetable basket.

Then one morning I had a new shock. Opening the two cabinet doors to get my bread out, I found to my disbelief the plastic envelope torn and a large chunk eaten out of my loaf. I stared with open mouth because it just didn't seem possible. The bread box was half way up the cabinet and behind the heavy drop flap. Since it hadn't been entered from front or sides, there was only one answer and sure enough further investigation revealed a hole about six inches across which had been chewed through the hardboard back.

The cabinet stood about three inches from the wall. The little devils must have ascended this narrow cleft, hung there and gnawed through the perfectly flat surface. And on a quite large and apparently featureless expanse had done so exactly behind the one spot containing reachable food! You've got to hand it to rats, and if you don't they'll probably take it for themselves.

I also had a separate fridge for dog meat standing in the conservatory – no problem for my little pals. They ate their way in through the pipes at the back and helped themselves, so that was the end of that.

All this time my temptingly baited breakback trap sat, virginal and deeply ignored beneath the washbasin beside the little tub still continually overturned. A stool stood between the bath and the washbasin and it occurred to me that the longtailed athletes erupting from the cupboard might be jumping straight on to this instead of into the bath. One evening therefore I put the trap on the stool and bingo! Within fifteen minutes I heard a snap and there was a rat – dead, thank goodness. My first victory since Nobby had shot the young female in the cage.

No two ways about it, I had to get rid of these creatures, yet even now I think of that rat with respect. For it was more handsome than any wild rat should be. So big and wholesome looking, with a glossy soft brown coat and even a pretty, curvy, creamy shirt front. He looked like an illustration from a child's book, more Mr. Fox than Mr. Rat!

I sent for the council ratman – rodent operative to you. He and his sidekick were suitably impressed by my victim and obligingly disposed of him for me. They agreed with me on the route of ingress but told me that they were not allowed to block it for me – surely one of the dottier of council regulations. I would have to do that myself. They were only allowed to lay poison.

They agreed that nothing must be laid on my premises, to protect the dogs. Instead they went next door – which was then empty after the deaths of Tom and his wife – and laid bait liberally inside the drains and two of the old garden sheds.

A week later they came to clear it away. It had all gone and they found the remains of at least a dozen rats, while I took three corpses away from some rather peeved dogs. The rats of course were from the surrounding farm and woods, and I wish they had stayed there, not come muscling into my house, as I hate killing things.

This was satisfactory but still left me with the problem of stopping their entry. All or nothing – I mixed a bowl of concrete, climbed a ladder and filled the whole space on top of the conservatory framework from the hole in the roof to the first crossbeam.

This denied them a foothold from which to work. Otherwise I was by then convinced that they, like the heroes in some film of derring-do would find some way to move the stone from the mouth of the cave and be back in business. This time it was I who won, and there has never been a rat in the house since. But my semi-superstitious respect for the tribe persists.

Did the knowledge of their old trade route die with that generation or will its existence, as a legend of old, still be carried in some ratty Iliad told by grey-whiskered elders to the young and ardent ratlings in the ancestral hole and inspire rats yet unborn to storm the citadel?

12

From Bog To Bathroom

So at last my house was rat-free, and looking with loathing at my abysmal bathroom, I decided to take the plunge. So much was wrong with it that it was like one of those television programmes on How To Sort Out An Awful House.

The bath itself was not at all bad, being cast iron. I didn't want to change this as a fibre-glass one might not stand up to the wear and tear of dogs being bathed in it, without becoming badly scratched. This bath was white, so no chic coloured suite for me.

I also had a nice white porcelain basin donated by a customer who had recently changed her own bathroom. This was a big improvement on the cracked and ugly one I had inherited with the house. The lavatory itself, although clean, was old and had a simply hideous high-level cistern and chain which might have come out of my old Bermondsey infants' school half a century before.

Fortunately I was in funds after the sale of a big litter of puppies, and as usual looked around among my customers for help. It is impossible to speak highly enough of the support I so often received from this source.

As well as friendship, advice and actual practical assistance, they provided a generous stream of items that admittedly they no longer wanted but which were nonetheless welcome.

I had come into my cottage with only a very basic assortment of household items, and in the years that followed often used to look around and think that nearly everything I owned had been donated by some kindly owner of a dog I had trimmed.

So it was now. I didn't have far to look, for one of my customers was an elderly retired builder who seemed to know the crafts of his trade from A to Z and who was taking a little private work. He willingly agreed to come to my aid, and in fact rang me a week or two before he was due to begin to say that he had just removed a white loo with low level cistern from a house he was renovating and I could have it for a fraction of the cost of a new one. It was good porcelain and he was rather scandalised at its previous owner's insisting on replacing it with coloured plastic.

Of course I accepted and he duly brought it along. In one day this bewhiskered angel had installed both loo and wash basin, replaced the flaking old bath taps with a plated mixer set with shower attachment (also donated by a customer) and, wonder of wonders, actually stopped the hot water from overflowing.

This last feat might not sound much, but that overflow had been running for at least twelve years and had defeated the best efforts of four other plumbers. My friend simply spotted that the feed was equal to mains pressure rather than the usual gravity flow and changed the valve accordingly. Since the old lavatory had also overflowed with almost equal persistence I now had high hopes that the wall might actually dry out.

Not content with working these miracles, he also gave me some invaluable advice on other related problems which I followed slavishly. One recommendation was that I lay ceramic tiles on the floor and this I embraced enthusiastically, for what could be nicer? I love tiles and can buy them with the same fervour as other women buy hats.

This brought me joyfully to the question of colour schemes. I had always had a yen for a pink and grey bathroom and you might think it would have been easy to gratify. But is a strange thing that as soon as I am in a position to buy some perfectly ordinary item, it disappears from the shops. So it was now.

No pastels, I was told disparagingly, it's all earth colours now. Browns in every shade, yellow, orange and sultry reds. Nothing in pink and positively nothing in grey. But I wanted some pink in my bathroom, to me it is a gentle colour and gives a hint of warmth which is important to a chilly person like myself. I object to being bullied in the name of fashion. Mulling peevishly over the colour schemes displayed, I decided I would have none of them but see which individual tiles took my fancy.

Browsing among the floor tiles, I fell for a line depicting the leaves and prickly fruits of the sweet chestnut and chose it in the darker brown version. An earth colour, I admit, but a lovely rich warm one to cheer the heart.

Having white porcelain fixtures, I was a little restricted in my choice of wall tiles, but made a virtue of necessity and chose white as an integral part of the scheme. I fell for some showing bold white ripples on a pale biscuit ground.

Better still the decorative ones accompanying them had water lilies floating on the ripples. I wasn't to be cheated of my pink, though, and the choice of a pretty pink-flowered paper sporting biscuit-coloured foliage warmed the whole ensemble nicely.

I didn't buy all these things at once. Having been assured that the tiles were a new line and would be available for some time, I used to drop into the shop and buy as many as my purse would run to every time I passed.

The fervour of artistic creation which all this induced now acted as a spur to give me that genuine urge needed to launch me on to the sea of effort required to get the job done.

It was at the beginning of a halcyon year of sun and heat wave, and this was a big help because, once I had peeled off the remaining rags of wallpaper and shovelled the curling plastic tiles off the floor with the garden spade, the bathroom, reduced to its bare bones, began to be a cool and pleasant place to work in.

The bare brick walls were virtually innocent of plaster – a few knobs and streaks of it persisted here and there – and I did not try to knock them off as I realised they would be useful to key the new surface to the wall. I needed to apply this as a backing for the tiles.

The walls were not too daunting a prospect, but no way could I make my wet cement mixture cling to their vertical surfaces for more than six inches without falling off. It helped of course to have the aforesaid knobs and streaks, and I could poke it into the holes.

The face of the brickwork was about as smooth as an eiderdown, and when I really got down to the job I was dumbfounded to discover daylight showing through in many places. No wonder the wallpaper was damp – the overflows had been running right through the walls.

It became a regular early morning chore to mix a load of cement and apply the daily ration of six inches to the two outer walls. Luckily the walls were neither long nor high. It looked a bit odd when it was finished as it clearly showed the irregular wavy tidemark of the succeeding layers, but at least the use of a wooden straight edge had given it a reasonably flat surface.

These walls were only one brick thick and no doubt this had contributed to the lacy effect. Strengthening them in this way was very satisfying and I used a lot of Unibond in the mix on my builder's advice. Plastering them was beyond me but anyway I intended to cover them entirely with tiles or thin polystyrene sheeting.

The floor too needed a thin skin of cement to flatten irregularities left after the revolting old vinyl tiles had been removed. Now my beautiful ceramic ones could go down. Not as easy as it sounds – the loo being in use, stepping stones had to be laid which then had to have tiles slipped between them after the first lot had set firmly enough to walk on.

This required careful spacing but was completed successfully in spite of my congenital difficulty in measuring anything correctly. Once done it was heartwarming to see their colour and pattern, the first flowering of design in this dismal room.

The next thing was the excitement of tackling my water lily lake. I decided to tile all round the bath and across the back of the basin and loo to a height of about four feet. But something else needed seeing to first.

While I was pleased enough with my iron bath it did sport some green stains below the taps – more long-term drips no doubt – and a nasty limestone scar at the other end caused by it standing on a slope so that the water never drained out completely.

The end of the bath would have to be raised so that the top edge was level, and it looked as if some broken roof tiles would be just right to push under the two legs and keep it there.

The only snag was that cast iron baths are very, very heavy. I summoned Dot and together we heaved. Calamity! It was impossible to get a good grip and our combined efforts couldn't even make it tremble.

But nil desperandum – inspiration struck. I went out to the car and returned with a jack. That did it. The broken tiles were slipped into position, the jack removed, and my spirit level confirmed that the top was level. This gave me a splendid line to begin tiling the wall, and before long I had my water lily lake gleaming in all its glory. I tiled the bath panel to match.

Some of the spare ripple tiles, cut in half, made a neat ceramic skirting for the remaining walls, so that it would be easy to wash the floor without marking the wallpaper.

The next job was to paint the woodwork very pale pink. Besides the old plank door, which I liked as being a genuine survivor from the house's original days as a labourer's cottage, the room has two very small windows, also survivors of its days as a coalhole and outside toilet.

There were still too many pipes wandering about so I painted them pink too. Some years later the house was re-plumbed and most of these disappeared. What an improvement that was!

Before putting up my pretty paper, I lined the walls with sheet polystyrene to withstand any remaining chill. It looked satisfyingly attractive. Now from donated wood I built a vanitory unit around the basin, with a cupboard underneath for cleaning materials.

I had been using a big plastic bin, bought from the village bakery for a few pence, as a laundry basket, and this I now covered with wallpaper to match the rest of the room. My wooden clothes horse, kept in the bathroom, was also painted pink.

All this added up to an unusual colour scheme of pink, white and brown which was pleasant, being both light and warm. I added a mirror and a medicine cupboard on the walls, a long pale shelf over washbasin and toilet, and lastly a fluffy white bath mat to complete the décor.

I felt very proud of my efforts. It was clean, it was bright, it was warm, it was practical and above all it was dry. Not a bad transformation for a dank chamber made out of a coalhole and an outside loo!

13

Sunshine And Socks

Of all the dogs I have had, I think the two who were closest to each other were Sunny and Socks. They were almost sisters as they both carried two lines back to my original bitch, the sainted Bamu. Curiously enough Sunny was extraordinarily like Bamu in type and temperament, while Socks reminded everyone who had known her of Bamu's daughter Toffee, who had nearly driven me insane with her compulsion to tear at speed all over the English countryside.

Sunny, well named Sunshine, was a dear little dog and very much like Bamu her ancestress who was my first Airedale bitch and the founder of my Caterways strain. When she first came to me, Sunny was as mischievous as a puppy could be – spreading a packet of milk powder evenly and impartially all over my sitting room – running along a window ledge and breaking a valuable vase, etc – and it looked like the start of a prolonged battle.

But after just three weeks, Sunny obviously thought that she had been everywhere, done everything and bought the T-shirt. In an overnight conversion she became a reformed character and was never naughty again. Gentle, loving, happy and intelligent, she was a joy to have around. No wonder Socks loved her so much.

She did have one problem – she was just terribly car sick. This was something else she shared with Bamu, but the one tablet for this malaise which had worked on Bamu was no longer available. The more I tried to get her used to the car the worse she got until the day when she was sick four times and had her bowels opened as well, during a five minute drive.

Appealed to for help, the vet gave me Largactil tablets and told me to give her one every day and then take her for a short drive. I believe Largactil is no longer permitted for this purpose, a great pity because it did work. Eventually we were able to leave it off entirely, and Sunny became so good a traveller that she could ride all day and if necessary be fed in the car without any unfortunate repercussions.

She grew to love the car as much as the other dogs did, and took a keen interest in our progress. The rear view mirror showed her standing behind me in the minivan watching the road as we passed and balancing easily against the bumps. If we got stuck behind a lorry, she would pay close attention and as soon as we pulled out to overtake and get ahead her tail would wag with triumph.

But the sight of any animal would be greeted with screams of excitement. This hepped-up reaction to car travel must have been a last remnant of her juvenile carsickness and never left her. The screaming-when-I-see-it phase only lasted about ten minutes and after that she would travel quite sensibly until ten minutes before we reached our destination. Don't ask me how she knew. Familiar journey or strange, short or long, ten minutes before we stopped, Sunny would be in full voice and excitement again.

Socks was never far from Sunny and constantly expressed her love in a hundred funny little ways. If she came into a room where Sunny was sleeping, she would position herself carefully to lie down so that their heads were together, then with persistent nudging and gentle tossing of her head would eventually wake her sleepy sister.

Always too good natured to growl, Sunny, after a few ineffectual attempts to go to sleep again, would obligingly begin those ministrations Socks craved, delicately licking and cleaning her eyes and ears. Socks would wear an expression of utter bliss while this was going on and at last, head to head, they would settle back to a companionable doze.

Sunny had five litters and was always a sweet and loving mother. Her first had been five puppies, then six, then eight and then eleven. The final litter numbered twelve. Sunny was so small, with a short back, so how could she find room for so many? Don't forget that each was attached to an afterbirth nearly as big as itself, and in the event we discovered that she was also carrying a very large quantity of fluid.

She was like a barrage balloon and appeared about to pop. As her pregnancy advanced, she became so uncomfortable it was pitiful to see her. She had difficulty in either sitting down or getting up and had no chance of climbing our steep stairs. She could not even turn round. If she was at one end of the room and wanted to come back, she would walk backwards.

I put four sprung settee cushions together to form a square on the front room floor and laid a rug on top. Before I went to bed I would pick her up and lay her gently on one side, where she would sleep without moving until morning. It was even difficult to feed her as much as she needed because she simply didn't have room for it.

When the day finally came, I thought she might have trouble whelping, especially as she was so tired before she began, but luckily the pressure within shot the pups into the world in record time – the latecomers in the queue were obviously pushing and shoving to get out.

I reared eleven of these twelve. Sunny was so exhausted by then that she could probably only have fed two or three unaided so I really had my work cut out supplementing the whole bunch, and at the worst of the weaning period was spending eight hours a day just feeding and cleaning the entire family.

Socks was a big and colourful Airedale. Her coat grew very thickly with magnificent swanky culottes so that, when she was in full coat, I called her 'Old Bushy Bottom'. As she matured, her colour became a glorious red grizzle. Head and legs were the usual tan, but on her neck a rich mixture of red and black hairs gave way to a perfect jet-black heart stationed on her withers, and behind that rippling waves of real red-setter red clad her body, only forking to a small swallow-tail on her rump to make way for her bushy tail.

In full splendour, combed out and fully groomed, she was like some superb walking chrysanthemum. I used to tell her 'You're like a flower, old Toffee-Socks' and she would grin and simper at me, for like many another fatheaded dog, she was immensely conceited.

Socks's heart murmur was discovered when she became very nervous at the age of eighteen months. Typically odd, she chose to be frightened of things overhead, trees blowing, street lights and so forth, and after I installed two new lampshades in my bedroom it took me a fortnight to persuade her to go in there.

Full marks to my vet for spotting the cause which was quite unsuspected by me. Heart tablets wrought a miracle cure. She was to stay on these for the rest of her life, and the edict was – no puppies. This didn't particularly worry me as, in spite of the financial blow, I knew that visually Socks was no credit to her breed apart from her remarkable coat. Logically I should have found her another home, but who would take a dog with a bad heart?

Socks was a comical creature. One of her little personal idiosyncrasies came on quite early in life and stayed with her till the end. She began to howl in her sleep.

Anyone who has experienced this phenomenon will sympathise with me, for the howl of a sleeping dog must be one of the most ghastly sounds known to man, and bears little relationship to the cry of the same animal when awake.

When Socks indulged she gave it her all and, as I was then sharing a house with other people, I had a problem. It was no good speaking to Socks or even shouting at her. While she was in full song I doubt whether you could have woken her with a megaphone even if you had it at her ear.

No, she had to be touched, even shaken, and it had to be done quickly before the police arrived and probably the army, air force and fire brigade as well.

Reluctantly I decided she would have to sleep on my bed. The reluctance was all on my side. Socks thought it a wonderful idea. She chose a spot by my right foot and kept to it from then on, soon joined by Sunny at my right shoulder. This gave me all the left half of the bed to kick about in and explains why I've stuck to a double bed ever since – one that will go up the narrow stairs.

I naturally asked my vet's advice but he only laughed and said Socks's nightly choir practice was the result of an over-active brain. He thought she was very intelligent and called her his favourite patient. I can't think why.

However our new sleeping arrangements worked. One howl from the foot of the bed and I would sit up and shake her by the shoulders. With a great gasp she would half wake and sink back to sleep with not so much as a startled glance.

No matter what her nightmare, you could rely on Socks never to resent a bit of rough handling in this emergency. That was one thing she certainly shared with Toffee, a quite bomb-proof sweetness of temper.

I expect it was this quality, combined with her clownishness, which appealed to the vet, because Socks was really a most hair-raising animal to take to the doctor's. This was one place she adored attending, for the exciting party in the waiting room. For that is how she regarded these gatherings.

She was perfectly certain that all these agreeable people and their dogs had come simply to see and admire her and she lapped it up. Then would come the summons to enter the consulting room and she would tow me in enthusiastically.

There would be her dear vet, whom she loved and admired so much, and a delightful young lady kindly acting as nurse so that she might be on the spot to minister to her, Socks's, lightest whim. Socks swam in a sea of euphoria.

Then would come the snag. Acting on hard-won experience I would heave her on to the table and everything would change. Once up there the mere fact that the vet had turned to look at her was enough to start her screaming like a banshee, and if anything in the least bit painful was attempted she would throw herself all over the table in the effort to escape.

I learned a few useful wrestling holds, and reinforcements would be called for from the animal nurses until there was barely enough room on her carcass for us all to get a grip, but she was still a pretty good match for us. And the noise was deafening. I used to try to be last in the waiting room out of consideration for the nerves of the other clients.

Socks was the only one of my dogs whose claws I have been unable to clip myself. I could put her on the table and tie her head in tightly, but her convulsive plungings and whoopings made it impossible to do the job without damaging the quicks – and if that had ever happened I don't know what the effect would have been.

So I had to ask assistance of the vet. He knew his patient and saw nothing ridiculous in my pointing out her longest claws. He always did these first and could usually get four or five done before hysteria set in and the operation was abandoned.

Once Socks caught her ear in the car door and it bled profusely. As I drove her slowly to the vets, I expected my car to be a puddle of blood, but received unexpected aid from Sunny, who stood patiently behind her injured sister and gently licked the wound all the way to the surgery. There the wound was stitched under anaesthetic.

When the time came to remove the stitches she was delighted to be back. Did they want her on the table or on the floor, I asked?

'Better have her on the floor and all sit on her,' replied the vet. I backed her into a corner, stood astride her and wrapped my arms round her neck. Two nurses came in to hang on other bits of her and the job was done to constant howling.

When Socks was seven she had to be spayed. That, I felt, would cure her of her delight in going to the vets. Not a bit of it. On returning to have those stitches taken out, her greeting was as fulsome as ever and she tried to pull towards the hospital section where she had recovered from the anaesthetic.

This time also she was kept on the floor for stitch removal and her voice proved as fine as ever. The vet ended up on his back on the floor, stoutly contriving to extract stitches rather as if he were working under a car. As soon as he had finished, Socks put on her usual post-consultation show of relief, rushing round madly to lick every person within reach and crying loudly 'Oh it's all over and I'm all right. Oh I have been brave, it was simply terrible, what a very brave dog I am! Aren't you glad?'

Really it was no wonder the vet had such a soft spot for her, especially as he said that if she had been a biter she would have had to be anaesthetised every time he saw her. But no matter how much Socks was beside herself with fear and hysteria, it simply never occurred to her to bite anybody at all. She really was an old poppet.

I never expected Socks to make old bones, and once she turned nine I always seemed to be making emergency rushes to the surgery with her.

One afternoon I had a standard poodle in for trim and shampoo. This was a very long job as the dog took me three quarters of an hour to collect, then it had to be rough trimmed, bathed, combed out and dried, re-clipped tidily, and then taken home again.

On switching off the all-obliterating drier, I heard an amazing sound. It was exactly like the noise of an old Puffing Billy train getting up steam to chug out of the station. But it was coming from Socks. Running in to her, I found her unable to stand and with her sides bloated.

It was nearly half past five. Ringing the vets, I explained my predicament and asked that someone would see her should we arrive after the surgery had closed. Reassured on this point, I finished my poodle in record time and rushed out into the darkness to get him home.

When I got back, it was a really nasty evening, dark, cold, and sleeting hard. Entering the house at the gallop, I opened the back door for the dogs to go outside while I shot into the bathroom.

Coming out again, I found to my horror that Socks (who I thought could not move) had gone out with them. I called. They all came in – except her. For the last week or two she had taken to lying under the willow and being hard to move, in the manner of many dogs who know they are nearing the end.

I went out again with a torch, but she was not under the willow. My garden is both large and pretty wild. I began to hunt along the fences, round bushes and under trees, calling all the time, but it was nearly fifteen minutes before I found her.

There was an old tumbledown shed in the wood just outside my boundary. I had been given permission to use it and had made a way through the fence. However I had given up this practice because the dogs, ratting, had dug a large hole in the earth floor. Also I was wary of my younger ones escaping into the wood via the broken window.

And there was Socks, lying nose down in the dirty hole and obviously with no intention of ever coming out again. It took me another ten minutes to drag her out and get her on her feet. Her breathing was terrible.

Supporting her with one arm round her rib cage, I took her through the drive gates and into the van via the back doors, giving thanks for the mini's low floor. Another fifteen minutes to drive to the vets as fast as could be, consonant with giving my poor old friend a smooth ride, steady on the bumps and easy round the bends.

Once at the vets, the combined efforts of myself and the nurse could not get her to stand. Her old friend the vet came out. Her sides were now bloated and hard, and her breathing could be heard all over the building.

'I shall have to operate at once. We'll take her downstairs', he said, picking her up bodily, and down we went to the operating theatre, but just inside the door she collapsed again on the tiled floor.

Oxygen was brought but fifteen minutes showed no improvement. I suggested that some of the wind might be broken with peppermint. He brought some in liquid form, and lifting her head began gently trickling it into the side of her mouth. Getting the taste, she lifted her head to splutter and that was all it took. Socks was gone.

I grieved for Socks and I grieved again for the mother lost again in her daughter. Socks had always been a sort of joke dog and for all serious purposes was pretty useless, but these oddball dogs have a charm and an appeal all their own because they are irreplaceable.

I'm wrong to say she was useless because she did have her little triumphs. There was the time she caught a mouse on the hearth, the time she wouldn't let Dot go upstairs because I wasn't there, and her pleasant habit of searching the darkening garden for sleeping puppies.

Sunny Sunshine must have missed Socks but did not seem to pine for her. There was an excitable side to her nature. When guarding the front fence, she would dash barking up and down, changing direction on a sixpence so suddenly that she more than once came in with her stopper pads bleeding.

Surely this must be how these appendages got their name, although it seems to be fairly rare for any dog these days to apply the brakes so violently as to bring them into contact with the ground. Possibly it was a more common occurrence in times when dogs were used more often for hunting various vermin.

It was about this time that I parted with several full-grown dogs. Two were rescued Airedales which I had happened to be able to help and successfully rehome, and the others were two young bitches which I had reared for a friend who was temporarily overstocked.

These transactions were all in the day's work for me but they had a far more sinister meaning for poor Sunny. With the Airedale's uncanny sense of what was afoot, she knew when people came to buy, and began to make herself scarce, keeping well out of sight until they had gone.

This was puzzling for she showed no signs of uneasiness when we had ordinary visitors but was as cheerfully delighted to see them as always. Light dawned – the poor lamb was afraid of being sold herself!

I'm glad to say that this wore off after a year or so, and it was probably very reassuring to her to be one of the squad translated from our old home to my new cottage. Anyway these fears seemed to dissolve and be forgotten, so my cottage weaved new happiness for her as well as for me.

What makes a dog a Very Special Dog? It is hard to say. I always feel guilty that I don't include Sunny in my list. Perhaps it is just that having so many – the total count is four – it just seems greedy to add to that number.

Sunny was completely devoted to me and had a very strong devotion to her home too, for whenever we came back to it she would have a little celebration all her own in both house and garden. Strangely enough, although she was the smallest and gentlest of my dogs the others all voted her boss, deferred to her and gave her pride of place. Socks of course particularly adored her but they all loved her, no doubt of that.

One night in her fourteenth year, she came to bed as usual with Socks and me, but seemed unable to settle. I concluded she must have a disturbed tum and took her downstairs to let her out. On her return she appeared not only to be in great pain but unable to change position from standing to sitting or lying down.

By four o'clock in the morning, Sunny was in a daze of pain and exhaustion – how long could her heart hold out against such an onslaught? Nothing for it but to ring the surgery. The vet suggested leaving it to five o'clock. Poor Sunny, it tore my heart to see her. At five I had to ring him again and by five thirty he was with me.

Examination showed that she was suffering from cancer of the glands with painful lumps that made movement agony. Extraordinary the way it just blew up like that in a matter of hours.

There was of course only one thing to be done and I was very thankful that owing to my vet being so caring she was spared many hours of agony. I asked him if he would put her in my puppy box away from the others, and he did. As I had to go out for a day's trimming, Dot and Nobby kindly came round and buried her in the garden in my absence and told me they had found her where the vet had laid her, curled up with her nose on her paws as if she were asleep.

As most of my dogs have been put down at the vets and left there for disposal, I was glad that Sunny, who had loved her home and family so much, was never to be parted from them but lies under the crab apple and the Queen Anne's lace at the top of her garden.

14

A Week In The Life Of

I was never short of work in those early years in my cottage and luckily I wrote an account of a week at that time which ran as follows:

Monday

5a.m. Am wakened by Sadie moaning downstairs. Spice is also squacking to be let out of her box. Well it's no use shouting at Sadie who is deaf, but it might be worth yelling at Spice. Since the house next door is empty, I am able to let rip with a mighty bellow and it works. The squacking stops. Sadie is still moaning but I turn on my one good ear – a technique perfected during air raids – and try to drift back into sleep again.

Even a completely deaf ear has its uses, but in spite of the blessed silence now reigning inside my head (if not outside) the growing light forbids sleep, and by six o'clock I am tottering precariously down the steep stairs.

I put down my torch, book and glasses and stagger through the milling dogs to the light switch on the far side of the room. Spice once released pops out of her box all a-wag. The five dogs accumulate in the doorway where their exit is barred by a wire panel. On the other side of this is Airedale number five, my puppy Shari, gracefully gyrating in her pleasure at seeing us all.

I remove the wire, not without difficulty, and unlock the back door. All six erupt with the force of an explosion into the back garden, where they rush madly to and fro, noses to the ground in case it has been invaded during the night. I shut the back door and stagger into the bathroom. Long before I am washed, dressed and compos mentis, Sadie is scratching at the back door. When I open it Shari, Storm and Saffron come in. Sugar is checking the front fence in case there is anyone in the lane who needs barking at and Spice has gone down The Hole. As it has been raining she is probably sitting in a muddy puddle down there, but what the hell, that's her problem. Sadie for some reason has been expecting the door to open on the hinge side – a delusion common in old dogs – and it takes her some minutes to realise her mistake, back out and find her way in on the right side.

By the time they have all come in and collapsed exhausted on all available furniture and dog beds, my breakfast is ready, so after shutting the back door I take it into the sitting room, where I eat to the sound of Radio One. Actually I probably hear very little of the programme because as always at meals I am reading a book. I get through an average of three a week, most of them my own property, read and re-read again and again so that my bookshelves have a very lived-in look. As soon as I finish eating, Storm comes up for the two teaspoons of coffee which I leave in my saucer. When she has finished she lies down again. I push my plate to one side, put my feet up and settle down to read for a few minutes because I am exhausted too.

All the dogs lie motionless and silent but I am conscious of all their minds concentrated upon me, because when I am ready to go, no matter how quiet and careful I try to be, the tiny snap of my glasses closing brings them to their feet as one dog.

Spice barks. All the Airedales begin wrestling, growling and barging each other. I'm lucky not to drop my crockery on the way to the kitchen, but once there I get out the big bin of dog biscuits and hurl six handfuls as far as I can in all directions. Once more silence falls except for the blatherings of the DJ and the soft crackle of dog biscuits breaking as the gang graze here and there around the floor. This is the start of the day, when my kitchen degenerates into nothing but a dogs' hash-house.

Sadie is not eating, I notice. In fact she has gone back to bed on the sofa. I divide a pint of milk between three bowls and crack an egg into each. I catch Sadie's eye, hold up one of the bowls and call her with a large beckoning motion of my hand. She climbs painfully down from the sofa, comes to me and puts her nose into the bowl. She loves her egg and milk and often goes without her biscuits while waiting for it, but this morning she does not drink. She looks apologetically up at me, turns and goes back to the sofa. I keep a low footstool beside it to help her climb up. She uses this gratefully and slumps back among the bits of old carpet which protect her favourite bed.

I consider the day's schedule apprehensively. Is this going to mean a visit to the vet? Ought I to ring up and see whether her own special vet will be on today? Sadie is thirteen and has a number of things wrong with her. I decide to wait and see what happens at dinner time.

The other two bowls of egg and milk go to Shari, who at six months is still growing, and Saffron who is pregnant. I divide Sadie's drink between the other three dogs and turn my attention to the washing up. This done, I get out the kitchen scales and put them on the table next to the pile of clean dog bowls and go outside to the dog fridge to fetch the meat and weigh out their meals, which will go into the cool cooker to defrost until wanted. But first Sugar, who has heart trouble, must have half her daily ration warmed up with hot water and fed now. Saffron too must have an extra bite for breakfast for her prospective family. Shari, as befits a growing girl, has the biggest dinner plus a helping of boneflour and cod liver oil, but Storm, biggest by far, must have a small one, only ten ounces of meat with a tiny sprinkle of biscuit meal because she is so liable to put on weight. Saffron has the regulation twelve ounces plus boneflour and cod liver oil for her puppies. Sugar's other half ration must also be weighed out, then seven ounces for Spice and finally Sadie's twelve ounces. Except for Storm, they all have an ounce of biscuit meal added to their meat.

The dogs are all roaming around looking expectant because I am stupid enough to toss each a scrap of meat before throwing the rest back in the fridge, but eventually it is all done, the scales wiped and put away, the carving knife and big spoon washed up, and last and most gratefully, my hands washed too. But I'm not finished yet. Sugar needs a heart tablet and this is given her in a piece of butter. Again everyone else lines up hopefully but they are disappointed as a second tablet and butter are slipped into Sugar's dinner and the oven door firmly closed.

Now there are water bowls to pick up, wash and refill. I get the biggest one filled and put down, and balance the next on the edge of the washing up bowl but the tap suddenly dries up. This means that the caravanners who have come for the apple picking are using the stock tap in the dip below my house.

I leave the bowl where it is and go outside. I need to get another slab of meat out of the freezer or there won't be any to use for the dogs tomorrow. At this point things are complicated by the arrival of Peanut, Spice's daughter, who lives nearby and comes for the day when her owners are working. She and Shari immediately start a running fight, but it is only play and I get the wheelbarrow and reluctantly make my way up the garden. The freezer is in the big shed which also serves as puppy kennel and is at present unoccupied. The trees and bushes bordering the path are overgrown and sopping wet. My feet get wet and my face and hands too. I grit my teeth and press on. There is trouble with the freezer because the thermostat is not working. In spite of it being loosely packed, I have to take an axe head to the dog meat before I can prise out a slab. I throw it gingerly into the wheelbarrow because this is a bundle of unbleached tripe, part of a consignment which arrived during the hot weather, and in spite of now being rock hard is definitely a bit smelly. It draws the dogs and they press lustfully round the barrow trying to get in a few crafty licks before I can get back to the house and toss it into the dog fridge. With luck it will thaw sufficiently to be used tomorrow.

The tap is now running again and the bowl overflowing. I put it down and the dogs queue up for a drink. The newspaper placed to soak up the drips is sodden. I roll it up with a shudder and replace it with a clean dry one. I have cunningly left a jug under the tap so that I am able to refill the bowls which by now are half empty again.

Bliss! Goodbye to all that until tomorrow! A time check shows that I have nearly an hour before my first customer arrives. As usual the place looks like a set for Steptoe and Son, but with all that time, who cares? I decide to do some washing so I fill the sink from the hot tap, stir in some Ariel and put my dirty clothes into soak while I vacuum. The cleaner will bring the added benefit that it will dislodge Shari and Peanut who are now having a lively mock battle under my favourite chair. This is all in good fun but unfortunately Peanut always fights emitting a ghastly yipping like a demented slate pencil, which rips my brain into a dozen pieces.

I start the cleaner, the puppies run out and fortunately I shut the door on them just as the phone rings. It is someone I have never heard of who wishes me to hand-strip her Airedale – which she didn't buy from me – 'any day this week'. I tell her civilly that I am fully booked and offer her an appointment in four weeks' time. During the next twenty minutes she tells me that she is going on holiday next week, that the dog is suffering from the heat, that she was given my name by somebody who knows me, that the dog is 'very thick', that her husband won't like it, that the dog is going into kennels, that she can bring it over by car, that she doesn't know what to do and that she will have to ask her husband. None of this provides an empty two-hour slot in my timetable so she rings off in an aggrieved manner, insinuating that a real dog lover would oblige to prevent suffering.

I rush around with the cleaner and hurl myself onto my washing. There should just about be enough time to put it through the spinner even if I can't hang it out, but when I try to rinse it the tap stops running again. This is too much, and cursing freely I turn the stopcock under the sink. This cuts off the supply to the field tap and restores my supply. When the sink is full. I conscientiously open the stopcock again. I hurriedly drag my bits and pieces out of the sink and on to the drainer to drip while I rush out to my workroom, and get the spindrier set up.

But it is not to be. Sugar, at her station by the front fence, sounds the alarm. My customer is ten minutes early and work – cash work, that is – has begun.

Treacle is one of Saffron's daughters and nearly two years old. She is a delightful little bitch with perfect manners, and so much like her great grandmother Sunshine, who died two years ago, that I wish with all my heart that I had never sold her. Her mistress stays to chat while I work and this is very pleasant. Unfortunately, however, it is early in the season and Treacle's coat is not at all loose. In fact, she has a brand new coat under a little rubbish. I peel the rubbish away and smarten her up considerably. I work extremely hard and my right thumb, which is soft after the summer's clipping, is quite painful but I am obliged to send her home with her new, and now shining, jacket intact. How can I charge full price? I can't, and despite my throbbing hand, make a 25 per cent reduction.

It is now 12.30 and I am about to leap into my car and drive to the village for milk and eggs when the phone rings. It is an esteemed old customer wanting his Airedale (which I bred) trimmed. I offer him the appointment for four weeks ahead and he accepts with many thanks.

Back from the shops, hoover my trimming table, etc. while the kettle boils, then a quick coffee and snack and another chapter or two to finish my Agatha Christie. Another bark from Sugar and my next customer has arrived. I dread this one, a maniacal cocker spaniel which I have trimmed for years because no one else will touch her. Her owner gives her tranquillisers before leaving home but never quite enough, so that she arrives feeling ill and minus any inhibitions against biting. We will truss her up as far as possible and Mum will don thick leather gloves to hold her. After an hour's screaming, snapping and struggling, we will be reduced to damp quaking jellies – while she will go away less the worst clods of mud and hair that she has accumulated in the last three months but far from as neat and tidy as I would like to see her.

After this the little poodle from the riding stables is a piece of cake, but first I must feed the dogs who have been shut in during the spaniel drama. It takes about ten seconds to grab their dishes from the cooker and put them down. They take about two seconds to clear them with the exception of Shari, who is not only a slow eater but likes to clean her dish exhaustively both inside and out.

I pick up the plates and wash them. The poodle's owner collects her, pays up, makes another appointment and departs with a few laughing remarks about her dogs and mine – she has five, mostly strays and unwanteds who have gravitated to her kindly shelter.

The washing is still on the drainer but I must pack up my tools and hoover the conservatory before I can spin it. Lucky in a way because I can suck the spindrier free of the dog hair which has inevitably drifted into the drum at the same time. Also it is now raining so I can't hang anything out but have to drape it over the clothes horse and various hangers. Business as usual – and it is years before I will get a washing machine.

I switch on the television and put my own dinner on to cook. Shari is being a pest, holding Sugar (her mother) firmly by the whiskers and wagging her whole body to and fro in an idiotic manner. I throw her out into the garden and follow myself with her chain collar and lead, dumbbell, blanket and a bag of chocolate buttons. Five minutes training follows, ending with a Send Away to her blanket, laid down against the side gate. As she is only six months I think she is very clever and am anxious not to overdo things or lose them by neglect either. She gets lavish praise and a goodly helping of chocolate buttons. When I open the door to go in, the others crowd out anxiously because they know the rule is that 'when Shari's been clever EVERYONE gets a sweetie'. Storm gets two because she is a little bit jealous. She is my Obedience star and isn't too happy about seeing her successor starting school.

Honourable debts discharged, I turn my meat under the grill and check the potatoes, then out into the garden to fetch coal and light the fire. Disposing of the ashes is going to be a problem. For ten years I have thrown them outside the kitchen door, but this summer I have transformed the bald dry plateau into a patio complete with some very nice furniture. This was picked up dirt cheap in an end of summer sale. Some jobs repay you out of all proportion to the effort made, and the smart furniture and neat paving slabs make my patio one of the nicest things I've done here. The news is coming on as I dish up my dinner so I don't hurry, being up to here with unions, Northern Ireland and politics generally. I am hungry, tired and badly in need of a sit down, so I carry my plate to my little table and sink gratefully into my armchair. I have just cut the first piece of meat when the phone rings. It is the woman who rang this morning, to tell me that she will take the appointment in four weeks' time. I try not to sound too pleased when I tell her that it has already been taken and that the next available will be two weeks later still. She says her dog can't possibly wait that long and rings off in a temper.

I turn the sound up again and go back to my dinner and my book. It's 'I Claudius' this time but I find I know it almost by heart and am only reading it because I wish the BBC would show it again.

Sadie is already moaning for her supper, but I make her wait till eight o'clock, when Saffron and Shari also share a pint of milk and a tin of rice pudding between them.

Tuesday

Much the same even to Spice waking me with her squacking. She is looking rather miserable and I realise she is undergoing a false pregnancy. All my bitches come into season together, practically on the same day, so I expect she won't be the only one with this trouble in the next week or two.

Today I have to go to Orpington where I have some customers. It is a pleasant morning as I am going to two of my favourites whom I have visited so long that they are both on their second poodles. One is a great gardener, and when we make our usual tour of inspection she gives me half a dozen cuttings of her choicest shrubs to see if I can root them. It's just as well she can't see my garden which has been neglected during the construction of the patio and has gone to weed in a big way. After she has restored me with coffee and sandwiches, I make a quick visit to the bank and do some serious shopping before turning my wheels homeward. I have barely got in and quelled the ensuing riot before my next customer arrives with another Airedale, coat also not loose, and I am hard at it for another two hours.

In the evening I get pen and paper and work out just what I am going to do with my Beginners class at the training club on Thursday. This way I can refresh my treacherous memory before I set out from home and with any luck will give a lesson with some sense in it. I take Charlie Wyant's book 'Heelaway Your Dog' to bed with me and do some serious study before falling asleep. Real experts are always fascinating. Charlie is no Graham Greene but I get the impression that, with a complete absence of preconceived ideas, he has learnt his training from his dogs themselves, and that is why it is so good.

Wednesday

Two poodles in a fairly distant village. I ought to have my head examined because how I loathe doing one of them, working in a dark, cold and incredibly dirty kitchen. The unfortunate dog not only matches his surroundings but twitches and trembles all the time, in unbearable pain from diseased ears. I have got more and more outspoken with the stupid owners of this dog, who always reply fulsomely how dearly they love him. Last time I was downright rude and glory be – it's worked. The poor dog has not only been to the vet but both ears have been operated on. Although still very apprehensive he may now have a chance and at least he can shake his ears.

It's a nice day when I get home so I go out and clean up the grass. I've got a lot of grass and six very productive dogs who seldom go anywhere else so this takes some time but I get it done. I look around in dissatisfaction. Last year the bathroom, this year the patio – next year I'm going to have a year just CLEARING UP.

I have to telephone various customers and also take a call from a woman interested in Saffron's forthcoming family. I open a tin of puppy food and set about worming the lot of them, crushing the tablets and mixing them with this tempting meat. I then just have time to pot up my cuttings before a customer arrives with two cockers, one with a light coat and one like a rug. When they are done, I pop them into my van to await collection, hoping devoutly that they won't mistake it for a loo. They don't, and after they have gone I spend a relaxing evening with Claudius and the telly.

Thursday

A big day with my pension in the morning and the dog club at night. Out of respect to the former and to increase my enjoyment of and usefulness to the latter, I try not to work on this day. When I say work, I mean trimming for money. I have been stripping Shari in instalments for a couple of weeks. Now I put her up on the table and finish the job. She is very dainty, with a beautiful head, and looks so elegant stripped of her wool. I put her down and she grabs one of her favourite toys – a long sock with a ball in the toe – and has a mad half hour, very pretty to watch.

Christina comes round with Peanut. She is off school with bruised ribs and a stiff knee acquired falling off a friend's bike. Christina is twelve and madly in love with all my dogs and proceeds to demonstrate how badly injured she is by chasing them all over the garden.

Storm will also be going to the club with us tonight so I put her on the table too, not without grunting as she weighs nearly ninety pounds and I am seriously overweight myself. She has a lot of leg hair and whisker and is quite hard to groom in spite of being angelic to handle. Quite devoid of bossiness in spite of her size, she is intelligent and loving. She has had forty children. Many of them have turned out very much like her and people still ask if they can have 'one of Storm's?'. Obedient and reliable, I feel that in her I have a rock to lean on. That's possibly all in my mind, but it's going to be a very black day when I lose her.

I tell her she can go, which she does, but not without giving me one of her quick impulsive kisses first. She bounces out into the garden and all the others come up to hustle her for showing off.

Sadie, who is eating normally again, is looking terribly tatty. I do her next, as well as I can, but she finds difficulty in standing on the table even with support. Then I decide to cut the grass while the weather is dry, but the mower won't start. I decide to remove the plug in case I have overchoked it. After a struggle I get it off and find to my satisfaction that it is oiled, and after I have cleaned and re-placed it the mower actually starts. Triumph!

Sadie's mother, Sunshine, is buried at the top of the garden. She was a very much loved dog and, as I drive my mower above the place where she lies, I say softly, 'Don't be frightened, darling, it's only me.' Idiotic, I suppose, but in a silly way it helps to keep her with me.

It takes an hour to cut the grass. I ought to clean the mower but usually put it away dirty from sheer exhaustion. The dogs don't like the noise and have all gone indoors, where they leap up and demand their food as soon as I join them. Christina and Peanut have disappeared. I feed the dogs, light the fire, have an early dinner, turn on the telly, put my feet up and try to catnap until it is time to wash and change for the club. Christina and Peanut reappear as they are also members and off we go. I stick to my old club, despite a forty minutes' drive, as I have been a member for a quarter of a century and regard it as my spiritual home. I take my class, using Shari and Storm as examples of before and after. I then work Shari in the next class which is taken by another instructor. She is too busy staring around her to work as well as she does at home but it is all good experience for her and she does enjoy it.

I spend another half hour chatting to friends and sorting out a little club business, then I have a progress test to judge. This brings the time to ten o'clock, so I gather my troops and drive home to deliver Christina to her family and get back to the dogs. Sadie has had her supper early before we went out, but Saffron and Shari have their rice and milk now. I stagger up to bed, where the pain in my thumb combines with overtiredness to stop me sleeping until nearly 2a.m. in spite of large doses of Ancient Rome.

Friday

Tina brings Peanut round early, before I have even weighed out the dogs' dinners. She asks if they can come to work with me today. She is still too badly wounded for school. Against my better judgement I agree, and phone my customer to ask if she objects. I know she won't. She and her husband are a very charming retired couple who have three dogs.

I am greeted with a sherry and coffee when I arrive and we are given a delicious three course lunch after I have done two of the dogs. I work outside in the husband's comfortable workshop while Tina chases the dogs all over the garden until my customer's husband takes a hand. Within two minutes he has her painting petrol tins, cleaning shoes and laying tables. She thinks this is great fun and puts her back into it with a will, never being short of energy so long as it isn't school.

To my dogs' relief we are home on time for their dinner. Since it is still a nice day I go out and begin clearing odd chunks of wood off an old shed, a gift from a friend, which is piled up in the grass. It has cost me £60 to have a base laid for this shed and it occurs to me that if it doesn't go up soon it will only be fit for firewood. Unfortunately it is too heavy for me to handle alone. I need male assistance.

Having been on my own now for twenty years, I have long since ceased to expect help to arrive and automatically plan my jobs single-handed. So after shifting the small pieces of wood, I haul out the door of the shed and prop it against the nearby kennel. To get out the rest of the shed front, I have to tackle the nettles with a grass hook, a painful job since they are taller than I am and of tropical profusion

The large back section of the shed is now at the top of the pile and this really is too heavy for me, but a stiff brush cleans it up and also the front and door. I get the creosote and lavishly paint all three. Of course it's impossible to get at the inside of the back section since it is still lying flat, but next time a male customer starts getting patronising about my efforts as a backwoodswoman I'll get him to shift it. This will expose the floor, which I can cope with, and that will only leave the two side sections, and not before time as they are fast sinking into the soil. In fact they look somewhat rat-bitten in places. I spill ample creosote on said places to discourage this, and go in to my tea.

Saturday

Shopping in the morning accompanied by Shari, Christina and Peanut. We go to the market and I buy a rather neat little trolley to assemble at home. Shari is still rather timid but is coping reasonably well with her weekly exposure to shopping in Tonbridge. I think she believes Peanut is there to protect her, Peanut not having a nerve in her body. Home to unpack and relax over coffee to read my Dog World and Radio Times. To my annoyance the BBC is showing the 'Day of the Triffids' on Thursdays – club night. Perhaps I'll get the book out. It's a long while since I read any Wyndham. Claudius has finally been deified and I'm now into 'Silas Marner', but it's as well to look ahead.

I really like to be lazy on Saturday afternoons but with a litter due in two weeks' time can't afford the luxury. The front room has to be cleared to act as nursery, so I spend some time shifting furniture to other rooms, taking up rugs and generally shunting things round. After my evening meal I spend a pleasant hour putting my new trolley together. It is aluminium and very light and will prove a terrific boon for years to come.

Sunday

Spice has been tearing chunks of hair out of her back and looks terrible, so after the dogs' hash-house hour is safely over I pop her into the sink and bath her, to her great disgust. She looks beautiful after this but has done too much damage to her coat for showing purposes.

I groom the dogs I missed on Thursday and then take my new trolley to the big shed and start bringing down the puppy box in sections. The trolley performs like a dream and I get everything down to the house, including the heavy pigging-rails, in three trips when it would have taken six or seven with the wheelbarrow.

I spend the rest of the afternoon getting things ready for the new family, first cutting two large strips of heavy double plastic from the roll given me by a customer several years ago. These have to be opened out by cutting down one side of the plastic tube and laid side by side on the carpet where they form a beautiful pale yellow damp-proof base which will last till the puppies go up into the big shed. Next come the back and left-hand sections of the wire puppy pen. One goes in front of the big bookcase so I prudently whip out my John Wyndhams first. Now I can erect the litter box itself. It has only been used once or twice and is very clean and smart-looking, especially when the pigging rails are put in. These are designed to prevent puppies being crushed between their mother and the sides of the box. I feel I've done a good day's work, and if Saffron's puppies decide to come before time there will be no need to panic.

All the girls come in and examine my work. With the exception of Shari they are all perfectly well aware of the meaning of this box and are keenly interested in the event.

I go out into the garden and look round me rather wistfully. It could certainly use some attention, yet the mown grass is jewel bright and the strong sunshine throws sharp shadows across it. My big fuchsia in a large pot placed strategically on the new white garden table makes a warm show of colour and contrasts bravely with the green.

It comes into my mind that all my life I have been making gardens, like bricks without straw, from rough neglected plots and with little money and less time. Some of these gardens have had their moments of beauty when I have been proud of them but always it has been my lot to be next door to some super gardener. Consequently whenever I have had a chance to show off to someone, that visitor has looked admiringly across the fence and said 'My word, your next door neighbour's got a lovely show', or words to that effect. Well, no one could say that now, faced as I am on one side by a jungle of weeds behind an empty house and on the other side by a tangled wood.

Sugar barks at the fence and the others take it up in chorus. It is two customers popping in unannounced to fix a date to have their dogs trimmed. I ask them in and the wife exclaims in delight at my patio which she hasn't seen before. Her husband puts his hands on his hips and looks around, shrewdly nodding his head as one who sees all the faults but is too polite to say so.

'D'you know,' he says seriously to me, 'This could be made to look quite nice.'

I pass.

15

Storm

I had been in my cottage just over a year when Sadie had her third litter – just two dogs and a little bitch which proved to be one of my Very Special Dogs. The days of Storm's life were some of the happiest I have ever had. They were also the days when I had more dogs than at any other time – five Airedales and one Dandie, or as I prefer to think of them, my five and a half dogs.

There were a lot of puppies bred and Dot and Tina were keen and frequent helpers. I was still going out to do much of my trimming, and got through several second-hand minivans in the process. When Tina and her little brother William started school, it was I who ran them into the village every morning and they christened my old van Speed Buggy.

They loved it dearly and never seemed to feel its inferiority to the more impressive vehicles in which so many of their classmates arrived – and Plaxtol even then was fast becoming a rather upper-crust place to live. For a time we had another little boy aboard as well, loose in the back with William. I suppose this would be illegal nowadays but no harm came to anyone and the kids loved going to school this way.

To say that I fell in love with Storm at the age of two days is no exaggeration. Indeed I wanted quite fiercely to keep her, yet so very nearly sold her while yet a baby. I was well aware of the dangers of allowing numbers to creep up to a point where it would be too expensive and too exhausting to look after my dogs properly.

At that time I felt that four bitches was my limit, and of the four I had at that time one was Socks, a permanent passenger. The newest was a young bitch with whom I frankly didn't get on. Although Airedales are usually confident and outgoing, this girl was really not happy here, easily upset and frightened and perfectly well aware that I found her irritating. It was a vicious circle but I felt the place was hers, and with a heavy heart I advertised my babies.

Sadie always had big puppies, and since there were only three this time they were enormous. Storm was a pleasure to handle, so solid and compact, and she was even more forward than her brothers. Most Airedales open their eyes at about fourteen days, but hers opened on the ninth and she promptly began playing, pulling her brothers' tails while they were still blind. Her teeth also came through early and by the time she was five months she had a complete set of strong white teeth which lasted all her life without visible deterioration. Her vet used to say that it would be impossible to guess her age by her teeth: even the points of her canines never wore down. This was obviously some pup and I yearned to keep her.

But I had to be practical, and the advertisements went out. At that time it was still usual to ask a little less for bitches than for dogs, but for Storm I asked the same as for her brothers – thirty guineas. A woman came to see them and said she would have her but only offered twenty seven. I refused, pointing out that I only had three puppies and only one bitch. She went away.

Then a miracle occurred, no doubt arranged by my guardian angel who saw me on the brink of making a serious mistake. I got a letter from some people who wanted not a puppy but a young bitch. They came to see my yearling and to my joy it was love at first sight on both sides. They took her and I am glad to say that she was a success from the start, and when she died eleven years later they wrote and told me that although they had owned other Airedales she was the one they would remember.

After she had gone, the twenty-seven guinea woman rang to say that she had decided to pay my price and I had great pleasure in telling her that the puppy was no longer for sale.

What an escape! So now Storm was a fixture, and over the years I refused many would-be buyers for her. I always told them 'You haven't enough money' and it is true that no offer would have tempted me.

Storm adored me single-mindedly and from her earliest puppyhood she wanted only to be with me and to please me. She was sired by Loudwell Mayboy who became a Danish champion. He was a very big dog, too big to get his English title, and all these three pups took after him. Storm just grew and grew, with massive bone and a noble head. She was rather long in the back and her tail was too curly for perfection, but I didn't care. For me she was without fault, and whenever I asked 'Who's gorgeous?', she would hurl her considerable weight straight at my chest.

I started Obedience with her and found she was very quick – unusual in so big a dog but a great advantage in Obedience work. She loved the club and rose steadily through the classes until she was our star pupil. Her main failing was that she didn't like carrying anything except the dumbbell and was liable to drop it on the way back, which made the Test A scent rather a toss-up.

On one occasion when we were in a match with another club – with A the top test – I thought I would make sure of it by buying her a little teddy bear, three inches high, to be her scent article. She loved this dearly but on the fatal night she went out soberly on the scent, caught sight of it and – 'Oh there's my teddy!' – she flung her forepaws in the air and pounced on it with joy, thereby losing all her marks, for as the judge said, she hadn't done a scent at all.

When I came to breed from her, she proved an excellent mother of large healthy litters. But immediately after one whelping, she became very ill, refused food and couldn't bear the puppies round her.

I allowed her to sleep on the sofa that night while I bottle fed the family. In the morning we went to the vet who found that she had a temperature of 106 degrees and, after palpating her, diagnosed a severe womb infection.

As he passed her where she stood on the table, she reached out and licked his ear. He jumped as if he'd been shot, thinking for a moment that she meant to bite, and gasped in relief: 'What a temperament! For a bitch who has just had puppies and is feeling as ill as this one to lick the vet who has just been examining her – what a temperament!' How right he was. Fortunately she made a swift recovery and was feeding her pups before nightfall.

Deciding to bath her one day, I closed the back door and prepared my bathroom, which is on the ground floor. The dogs were well aware what this portended and were all watching me nervously. When all was ready, I pointed a finger at Storm and said 'You!' She promptly turned tail and shot up stairs, where she faced me defiantly from the landing.

Being in a silly mood I knelt on the bottom step, stretched my arms towards her and cooed 'Oh Stormy, won't you come to your lovely Mum?' Whereupon she was so overcome with emotion that she hurled her ninety pounds straight down the stairs on top of me. We both collapsed, laughing and cuddling. But to my surprise, when I released her and staggered to my feet, she walked right through my sitting room, through the kitchen and into the bathroom, where she climbed into the bath and stood waiting for me. That's real love for you.

Storm adored the car and claimed the passenger seat as hers. But owing to her great size and the fact that it was a minivan, it was impossible for her to get her whole body accommodated. She solved this by resting her head on my left hand as it held the wheel, and we drove many miles like this, with my right hand doing all the work, allowing the wheel to slide through my left so as not to disturb her.

One night I believe she saved me from a nasty experience. We were driving home very late along a dark, narrow and twisting country lane when suddenly there was a vehicle right behind us and it was flashing its headlights up and down in an aggressive manner. My first thought was that he wanted to pass, my second that if I let him he could block my way and I would be helpless.

I was doing forty, plenty for those conditions, so I decided to keep in front till we reached a wider road. But it was unnerving. There couldn't have been two clear yards between the cars and the flashing continued.

I said to Storm, who was asleep in her usual position, 'Sit up, Stormy, and look out of the window.' Just that, but she immediately did what I asked. When she sat up, her head was higher than mine which must have surprised the following driver. He dropped back at once and the flashing stopped. If his intentions had not been criminal, why should it have mattered to him that I had a large dog with me?

On one occasion I had a visit from Mr. Izumi Takahashi, a Japanese chief of police in charge of that country's police dogs. He was a great Airedale enthusiast and I believe about a tenth of their police dogs at that time were of this breed.

He considered them superior to either Shepherds or Dobermanns in tracking and valued them particularly because, as he said, 'The Airedale knows the wrongdoer.'

Mr. Takahashi came to a training session at Bromley where as it happened we had several Airedales working. But it was Storm he was interested in and wanted to buy.

When I refused (politely), he asked through his interpreter that I would let him know when she next had a litter and he would take the lot. But Japan was having a very bad press in the dog papers, and I'm afraid he had no chance although I liked him personally.

Storm had five litters and, as she was so big and strong, I thought I might get a sixth. But when I had her checked by the vet before mating, he warned me that she had a heart murmur so that was out. She continued to be my constant companion, support and joy and to ride beside me wherever I went.

Strangely enough the two daughters which I kept, Saffron and Sugar, although lovely in their own ways, in no way matched up to their

The Sixteen (Kent and Sussex Courier)

The Hole

Saffron

Helping grandson Giles keep shop

Storm practising for the show (Sevenoaks Chronicle)

Enjoying the garden, 1985

Storm

Betty and Fred with Shanty in Yorkshire

Sunny and Socks on holiday in Yorkshire

With Spangles on the patio, 1985

Speed Buggy

Christina exercising happy dogs at Bewl Reservoir

Christina and Sunny at Windsor

Happy show dogs, Windsor

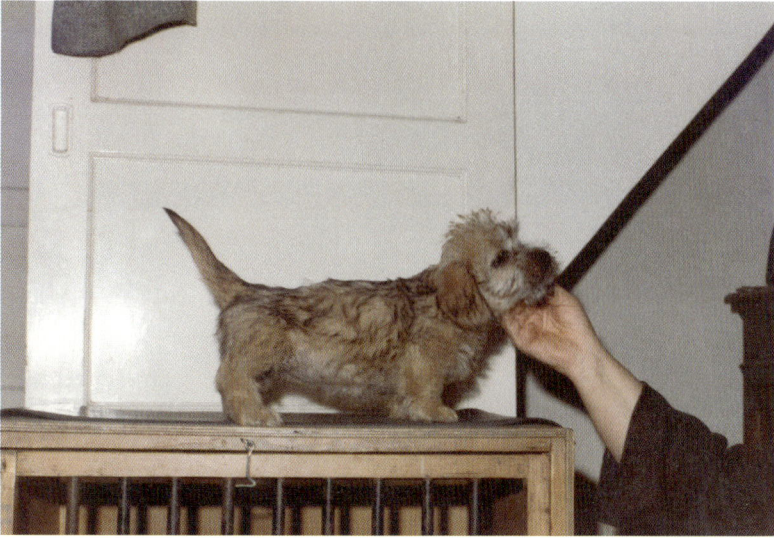

Spice on her box

Christina and Storm at Windsor

Trimming those fiddly feet

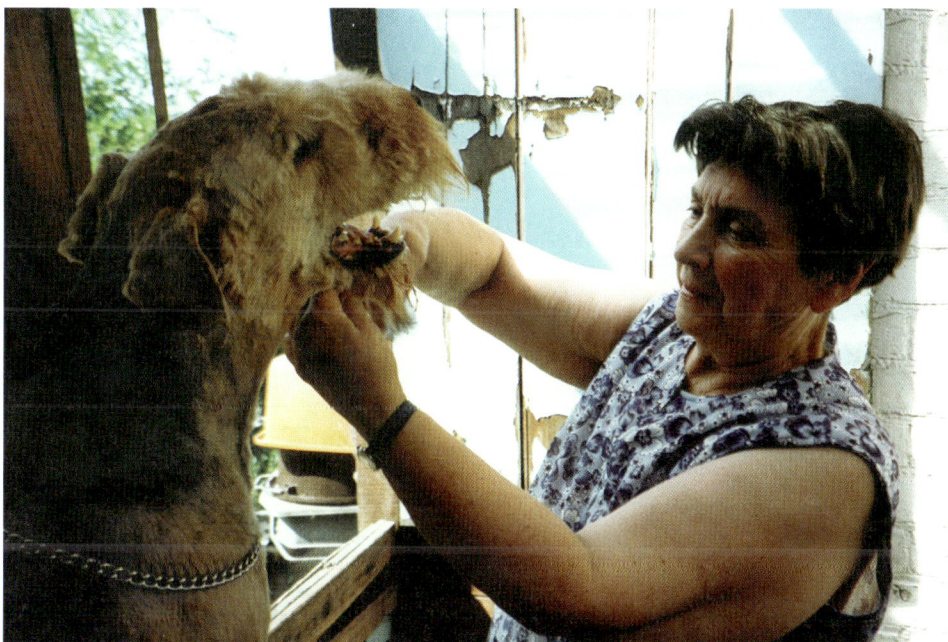

Perfecting the beard

Handwork is best

Next customer waiting

The keen gardener

Dora shuts the dogs out of the garden

Dora with young Scrumpy

Clarisse recuperating

Clarisse with young Scrumpy

Wonderful Heather

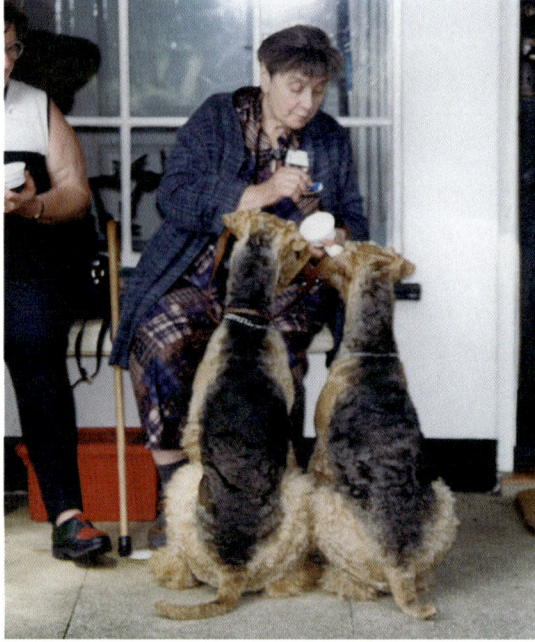

Two for icecream

Monica Dixon presents a cup to Dora

Lost in a wisteria jungle

With son-in-law Ted

Dora and the girls at the gate

mother and I had more pleasure from her two granddaughters, Spangles and Shari, the two 'young ones' mentioned in the poem 'Driving in fog'. I wrote this towards the end of Storm's life as I felt her powers declining, and it is strange that this drive in the fog was the very last time that I rode with her head on my hand. It must have become just too difficult for her to maintain her position and thereafter she lay in the back with the others. All her life I never remember her ever doing anything naughty, but I have some funny memories of her – like the time I heard her bawling for help from the garden and found that she had burrowed her way into the coal bunker. The coal had shifted and blocked her exit, and she was standing with her head and forepaws poking out of the top, feet black and face with an expression of dismay on it and the concrete lid balancing against the back of her neck.

When I acquired my Dandie, Spice, this little scrap had an especial affection for this biggest and kindest of all the Airedales. Having finished her own dinner, she would walk through Storm's back legs, stand under her chest, poke her head through her front legs and steal the food out of her bowl while Storm obligingly tried to eat what she could from the far side.

Storm was also chief architect of The Hole. With a little help from her daughters, this at one time had three entrances, went right under the tree and could swallow as many as three full size Airedales without trace. It was also much appreciated by gangs of puppies who would disappear into it as one pup whenever their elders set up an alarm.

She got a great kick out of putting on a show of rampant savagery whenever a horse passed our garden. Not only barking, but leaping at the fence and hanging on the top straining wire, which eventually she actually cut right through.

Came the day when the fence gave up and collapsed and she found herself out in the lane with the horses. Did she attack? Not on your life. Instead she ran straight to the side gate and requested urgently to be let back in. There's horses out here, Mum, and it could be dangerous!

Our club sometimes made an expedition to the Bedgebury Pinetum and adjoining forest with all our dogs, and as I was a slow walker I usually brought up the rear. But once when I was up with the leaders, I was urgently summoned to go back. Storm had come up, and failing to see me in my usual place, was standing stock still and howling most bitterly. My friends were astounded by such behaviour. I wasn't, and reunion restored her happiness at once. I may add that although instantly and completely obedient to me, Storm felt no obligation to obey anyone else. To her that was a completely different ball game.

Storm was ten when she began to fail. Indications were very slight at first, just a stiffness in the hind legs and some difficulty in climbing my stairs. She slept in my bedroom, where else?

At eleven she had to undergo an operation to remove a tumour from a stifle joint and I took the opportunity to have her spayed at the same time to remove the danger of pyometra. She made a perfect recovery, never even licking her wounds, let alone biting them – I am happy that I have never had to use the abominable Elizabethan collar. But her hindquarters grew steadily weaker and soon I had to climb the stairs behind her, part pushing, part lifting her.

I tried everything, including homoeopathy, to no avail. She who had always been so clean lost control of her bowels. The vet explained that she had no sensation there and it was obvious that she did not know she was passing anything. I adjusted routines and cleaned up after her, and when we went to the vets I took a large newspaper for her to sit on to minimise accidents.

On her thirteenth birthday, an Airedale-besotted friend came to tea and together we gave Storm a party. Two huge plates of fishpaste sandwiches – I did have six dogs – a big bag of meringues from the village bakery, a few chocolate biscuits and milky coffee for all. Every dog's face was a picture of delight and disbelief!

But a short three weeks later I had to go to a committee meeting. I shut off the access to the back garden as I knew that if she went out and collapsed I could never get her back on my own, but I left the door open into the conservatory. And there I found her, lying in her own mess and quite unable to get up on her poor wasted limbs. Cold, tired and frightened, how long had she been there? I knew then that I was being selfish. I cleaned her up and got her indoors and on the sofa. I slept in an armchair beside her that night and in the morning we made the last ride to the vet. Once she was on the table, that kind man made some excuse and went out, leaving us alone for ten minutes, when we said our goodbyes.

So what made her such a Very Special Dog? I've had better-looking dogs and I've had cleverer ones, and Storm never won a lot of prizes or did anything astonishing. But she was utterly reliable in everything she did. She gave me real support and unwavering love. There was nothing slavish about this, she was a real character who always maintained her self-respect and expected to be treated with respect.

But that love was always there, a tangible force, and she had generous and very individual ways of expressing it, burrowing her head into my lap with every sign of bliss, or walking between my knees, which was her idea of 'togetherness'.

She was just pure gold all through. I'll never forget you, Stormy. You're well entitled to your place up there with my other three Very Special Dogs, and I wish all who read this the same good fortune that was mine when I had you.

Driving In Fog

Old dog curled on the seat beside me
Stirs and takes her heavy head from my wrist
Sighs, moaning quietly with cramp,
Then stiffly climbs over the seat's back,
Absurd tail drooping, to drop her length
On the van's padded floor. On either side
Cushioned on ancient carpets, drunk with sleep,
Two young ones ignore their grandam's pain,
They think of nothing but the drumming movement,
And joy of travel fills their happy hearts.
Outside the fog presses upon my capsule.
I steer my spaceship through the hollow void
Past streaking meteors or yellow headlamps
And into vast black holes or cosmic woods.
Yellow and chill it lies upon my windscreen
Scarce wounded by the wipers' busy arcs,
The heater whirrs, the toiling tyres hum.
Coming from nowhere, heading for nothing,
The thin tin shell enfolds a fragile world,
Where careless youth still coexists with age
Whose frailties will surprise it too in time.
The rides we yet will take, your head upon my hand,
My hand upon the wheel, must have their number
And I must look to them to take your place.
But now, old friend, we still can ride together
Warm through the wastes of fog or Universe
Coming from nowhere, heading for nothing,
Lit by the by-pass' galaxy or Milky Way.

16
Dandies

I had previously had no experience at all of Dandie Dinmonts when a farmer's wife asked me to trim her new puppy. She did not want it clipped and I had no idea how a Dandie should be trimmed. We solved the problem by combining my techniques and the information in a reliable book she provided.

As we discussed this in a long sunny room filled with beautiful furniture, seven month old Shadow was busy playing. Round and round this enchanting little dog went, pushing the ball under each chair and dashing round to pounce on it on the other side. It is lovely to see a dog play happily on its own and from that day I had an affection for the breed.

Shadow proved to be a real little sweetie. She enjoyed her trims and grew very fond of me. After a while I suggested she might be worth showing, and thereby launched her owner on a new hobby. Shadow did very well indeed, and later her daughter Teasel did even better, becoming a champion and Best of Breed at Crufts. It was good to know that I had trimmed a Crufts winner.

I had long hankered for a small breed to add to my Airedales. Could Dandies be the solution? I considered carefully. The adult Dandie looks an oddity among dogs, partly due to the trim. That big cloudy topknot makes his head look so huge and everything is done to exaggerate his length and lowness to the ground. But his roach back largely protects him from the spinal problems of the Dachshund and the flatness of his big eyes makes them less vulnerable than the pop eyes of the Peke.

Above all, as with the Airedale, it was the temperament which attracted me. It came as no surprise to find that the two breeds are closely related, both being developed from the Otterhound. So despite appearances, for me the Dandie is the nearest thing in personality to an Airedale that you will find in a small dog, nearer even than the Lakeland and Welsh terriers.

They are named after the character Dandie Dinmont in Sir Walter Scott's novel 'Guy Mannering', a man who kept a pack of small terriers.

Only two colours are permitted, a grey called 'pepper' and variations of fawn called 'mustard'.

By now I was trimming several Dandies, all with Shadow's gentleness and sense of fun, but I did not find it easy to get a puppy. Dandies are not very prolific and none was available however hard I searched.

At this point my daughter-in-law, then living in Scotland, told me that an eighteen month old bitch was being advertised locally at a very reasonable price. She bought her for me and we arranged for her to be sent south on the Crufts coach in the charge of one of the exhibitors. I picked her up on arrival and was delighted to see a pretty face looking at me from the box. On getting home she and the Airedales hit it off at once.

I called her Silver as she was a pepper with a beautiful coat like a soft pencil drawing. I have never seen a better Dandie head: a face like a pansy flower, with huge dark eyes and a marvellous topknot of pale lilac hair.

Alas, it was all too good to be true. The sad fact is that although agile and energetic, she had the most atrocious movement I have ever seen. X-rays revealed she had suffered a spinal injury when a baby and could not risk having puppies of her own. Nor could I show her.

This was a blow, especially as Silver was so likeable. Even I realised it would be madness to take on another passenger for life. Luckily I was able to sell her to a good home for a nominal sum: one of my customers, a doctor, was looking for a good-tempered little dog as a companion for his mother. There were no children to pull her about and before long she was spayed, sparing her the dangers of a litter.

Feeling that her breeder (well known in Scotland) should know about this, I wrote and asked for her comments. She told me Silver's mother had been placed to have her puppies in a home where there were a number of children. It is not hard to imagine how she came by her injury. The expert demanded I send Silver back to use for breeding, inferring that my vet didn't know what he was talking about. The southern Dandie people were as disgusted as I was at this approach. I feel it is appropriate that Silver's breeder, by her uncaring attitude, lost what might have been the best specimen she ever bred.

Very disappointed, I ordered a bitch puppy with good temperament and sound movement from the Cornish kennel from which my customer's dog Shadow had come. I had a long wait but eventually a puppy was sent in a converted tea chest to Paddington, where I collected her and drove her slowly home.

My Airedales welcomed the new baby with enthusiasm: they seemed to think I had bought them a dog of their own. Their reactions were typical of each. Sunny thought she was lovely but made it clear that the real cause of rejoicing was still my return from foreign parts. Sadie (who hated puppies) turned away sickened. Storm thought the baby delightful, as did Saffron, but both soon lost interest. The real enthusiast was Sugar, then only six months old. It was obvious that this delectable puppy had been acquired specifically for her. She adopted her immediately and was very sweet with her new pet.

This promptly solved the name problem and now I had both Sugar and Spice.

To protect Spice from her boisterous companions and the moods of Sadie, I found a good strong box with a barred door. I installed this under the table and was able to shut my puppy in safely for the night. Sliding into sleep myself, I always knew she would be safe for the night.

This worked so well, and Spice liked it so much, she used it as her private room for the rest of her life – and to my amusement, when she died it was promptly claimed by Shari so I was stuck with it for the best part of twenty years!

Dandie puppies are incredibly pretty, with wide innocent eyes. Dot and Christina were instantly enslaved and Tina all but moved permanently into my home.

After my lifelong involvement with Airedales, I found it curious that so many people accused me of changing breeds, some reproachfully, others with congratulations. Often my accusers themselves had a second or even a third breed along with their favourites, but that did not stop them thinking that water was going to run uphill because Dora was going out of Airedales! However, the Dandie was only ever an addition.

I was very excited to breed from Spice as it was a new venture for me. It entailed driving all the way to Cornwall for the best match, when I stayed the night with her breeder and satisfied myself as to the desirability (in fact irresistibility) of her husband.

The result was a super litter of four girls and one boy. Thinking it best to space out my dogs, and that there would be chances later, I did not keep a bitch myself but did hedge my bets by giving one to Tina, then dogless. The arrangement was for me to have one of Peanut's puppies in time. Alas, Peanut never produced.

My Airedale Sugar had puppies at the same time as Spice and by five weeks both litters were in the garden, each in its own run. This was fine by Sugar, but must have worried Spice, although not on account of her own family. No, she obviously thought Sugar was not fit to be a mother, for to my surprise she took every opportunity to jump in with the young Airedales and feed them – ignoring the fact that they were all already taller than she. I have a photograph of her doing this, with an expression on her face which says clearly 'Well, somebody's got to do it!'

The bitch puppies of Spice's second litter died, and her third litter consisted of only one. I had every intention of keeping this beautiful little bitch. She was born on the first of April and so I called her Motley. Spice was a devoted mother, though with a tendency to protectively overlay her offspring. At four weeks, Motley was gasping for air and in a few days she had died. I just couldn't understand it and asked the vet for a post mortem. This showed that her lungs had been invaded by a horde of developing roundworms which had so damaged them as to make life impossible.

I blamed myself bitterly but in truth it was an understandable mistake. My dogs are routinely wormed twice yearly, and this had been done just before Spice had been mated so I thought it unnecessary to do it again. Wrong – for the hormones activated at this time awaken dormant worms which have been untouched by previous treatments.

Even this would not have done so much damage had there been other whelps in the litter. But poor Motley, as a singleton, had received the full force of these horrible parasites' attack with fatal results. The damage had in fact been done before birth. I felt so sorry for Spice suddenly deprived of her beloved baby, and as if all this were not bad enough, she never again became pregnant. I had lost all chance of founding a line on my dear little dog.

When Spice was ten she slowed down a lot and became very inactive. A check with the vet revealed that she was suffering from internal bleeding. He did an exploratory operation and found her stomach was so badly ulcerated that he had to remove part of it. Given only a 50 per cent chance of recovery, Spice came home to convalesce. She felt the cold terribly and I gave her a little tweed coat which I had originally made for Bamu. Despite this, to my distress she lost all her hair, revealing dark scaly skin.

The vet said not to worry and put her on thyroid tablets. The effect was miraculous. Not only did she grow a magnificent orange coat and swiftly regain her strength but I was able to increase her food considerably without her getting fat. It was probably her previous miserly meals which had caused the ulcers, the lack of bulk failing to absorb the acid in her stomach.

Fortunately she was still allowed her favourite titbit – orange peel. Dogs do develop these strange tastes now and again. She never ate the zest, but turned the scrap of peel over so she could nibble away the pith. It takes all sorts! She was thirteen when she died of lung cancer. I have never had a Dandie since, though often tempted.

For me a chapter had closed.

17

My Pair Of Cousins

After I had been in my cottage for about ten years, two of Storm's daughters, Sugar and Saffron, each presented me with a litter. Saffron was a good-looking little dog who had a blazingly vivid colour at a time when Airedales looked mostly rather faded, and who also bucked the general trend by having a really harsh pin-wire coat. For the first time in my life I was able to show a dog which could and did win, but this only lasted while she was in the more junior classes.

The trouble was that with such a hard coat it was not easy to grow good furnishings on her, and she was particularly short of whisker. This did not matter so much in puppy and junior, but when she was up against mature competitors she was at a disadvantage because not only did her head look short beside theirs but it spoilt the whole balance of her outline.

Sugar on the other hand was rather pale in colour and soft in coat, but more than made up for this by the exceptional sweetness of her disposition.

Both of these bitches were relaxed and good-natured girls. Neither ever did more than basic Obedience but they were always easy to manage.

Sugar once filled me with pride when she developed a bad aural haematoma, the ear flap being filled with blood and very painful. I took her to the vet with foreboding as she was then suffering from a severe heart murmur and I felt she could not stand a general anaesthetic.

My vet, sympathetic as always, used a local anaesthetic before slitting the inside flap to let out the blood. He then showed me how to squeeze out the matter which would surely accumulate and sent me home with instructions to do this twice daily after applying hot fomentations.

Being single handed, this might have presented a real problem if it had not been for Sugar's trust in me and her desire to please. So twice daily, I would make all my preparations and get everything together on a coffee table.

I would then sit down in an easy chair and call her to heel. She soon cottoned on and would come to sit close by my left side. Here, without even so much as a collar to hold her by, she would sit motionless while I did my stuff. Sweeties to end with, to be sure, but how many dogs would have put up with this treatment, which must have been painful, with such angelic submission? Sugar by name and sugar by nature, no argument.

She was a very sensitive dog and keenly alive to anything spooky on television, giving tongue on occasion in quite a distressing way. She particularly objected to broadcasts from graveyards and such places as the Valley of the Kings!

It is very interesting and curious, when you live with one family of dogs for a period of many years and generations, to see the odd little habits and talents which surface among them. Sadie could open doors, Shari collected emptied dishes, and Sugar also had an offbeat talent. She could unscrew things. This was demonstrated amply to me one evening when I came home after a day's trimming and found a new pint can of cod liver oil (bought for the current puppies) lying half empty on the lawn with the screw top beside it.

I picked it up, put the cap back on and restored it to its lawful cupboard. I had no need to ask who was the culprit for Sugar was curdled with guilt and could hardly bear to look at me. Until I had cooked my dinner, that is, and had just sat down at my little table to eat it, when she came pathetically to me, saying 'Oh Mum, I do feel ill' and promptly laid the missing half pint fragrantly on the carpet before me.

One of the features of my spring water supply in those days was that a single pipe served several properties. This meant that when one of the lower taps was in use the higher ones could get no water until it was turned off. But I had a tap under my kitchen sink which would effectively cut off the ones below me – the field stock tap and the pack house – and restore my supply.

Obviously I only used this when in real need and always turned it back on again as soon as possible. But one day I found the farmer's wife on my doorstep asking if I had turned off the water – the pack house was dry.

No, I said, then remembered that I had seen Sugar ferreting about under the sink earlier that day and went to check. Sure enough, the tap had been turned off. Hurriedly turning it back on, I went to apologise and explain what had happened. I regret that this was not well received. 'Hmp! A dog!' she said, walking off in disgust. She obviously didn't believe me and I couldn't really say I blamed her, except that I felt that if I had really been guilty I could have thought of a more convincing lie than that!

Sugar only had one litter because she found the whole process so upsetting that I thought it would be cruel to subject her to it again. I kept a puppy from this one and called her Shari, and a few months later she was joined by a daughter of Saffron's whom I named Spangles. Being so close in age they naturally became close in friendship and I always thought of them as my pair of cousins.

Even before Spangles's birth, I had begun training Shari and was amazed by her quickness and enthusiasm. What a joy to teach! She was retrieving at three months and doing Send Aways at five. Her heelwork too was the best I had had since my darling Solo, and I was in high hopes of having a real competition dog to work.

Alas, it was not to be. Shari inherited from her mother some odd quirks of nervousness. She was never afraid of people or dogs, but I have never had a puppy stare so at everything around her. It was almost impossible to get her attention. She also dreaded shops and warehouses of any description.

My lovely Shari – it can only have been this weakness which keeps her off the roll of my Very Special Dogs. She had all her mother's sweetness and at least twice her brains. In fact, she was one of the cleverest dogs I have ever had. It wasn't just her trainability, but she had an astonishing ear for speech. As she grew older, I found that I never had to give commands to her as such but just tell her quietly what I wanted and she would do it.

She was continually surprising me with what she picked up in ordinary conversation. I have never had quite this level of communication with any other of my dogs, with the possible exception of my first bitch, Bamu, and in Bamu's case it was all the more remarkable because she had been a kennel dog and very ill before I got her at the age of seven months.

There were a lot of generations between Bamu and Shari but I believe it was either a throw back or another example of those fugitive genes which run through a breed and are so difficult to produce on demand.

One thing for which I will always remember Shari was a trick which she thought up for herself and took enormous pride in. When everyone had had their dinners and finished polishing the dishes all over the place, Shari would go round and collect them all. I had five dogs at the time and the fun really started when Shari thought she had brought all their dishes in.

I would say – there's a dish missing – and she would start looking for it. 'Is it Sugar's?' I would ask, and she would run to the spot where Sugar usually ate – all my dogs had their own feeding stations. No luck?

'Look in the garden,' I would suggest. No luck again?

'She must have pushed it under the chair.' And sure enough, there it would be, to be hauled out in triumph by my dedicated helper. I often miss her assistance now when I have to go round all these places myself!

Storm died, leaving me with an empty space which has never been filled, and soon afterwards my friend Clarisse came to stay – a classic case of the visitor who came for a night and stayed for four years.

With her she brought her German short-haired pointer Clover, the colour of chocolate and timid and self-effacing. So much so that all my mob accepted her without the least trouble, and she soon became great friends with them all. In her former home, Clover had never been allowed to get on the furniture – in fact she was often kept in a singularly comfortless kennel and this was doubly hard on her because besides having a very short coat she was arthritic and had had rickets, the legacy of a puppyhood spent at the mercy of a cruel owner.

She was lucky indeed to have been rescued by Clarisse, who loved her dearly, and was obviously more than happy to be in my little house which is always warm.

Clover watched enviously when she saw my girls making themselves comfortable on the furniture, and one evening she crept slowly, quietly, guiltily, up on to the old sofa. I think she quite expected to be sent off pretty smartly, but instead we praised her for her bravery and congratulated her – and that was the beginning of a love affair for next to her Mum she loved that sofa best in all the world.

We were so lucky that from the time I first took Solo there for her first inoculations until the sad day that the last remaining partner retired, we had such wonderful service from our firm of vets.

Not only were they kind, competent and helpful, but there was always a welcoming atmosphere at the surgery and all my dogs loved going there.

At one time Shari had to be hospitalised and I was not happy about leaving her, knowing how she hated strange places and thinking she would be frightened as well as feeling ill. She was being treated by Irina, a brilliant young German vet who was then assisting the regular partners. I explained my fears but Irina assured me that Shari was feeling too ill to take much notice of her surroundings.

Two days later, I got a phone call from Irina – 'Shari says she would like to come home, and I've told her she can as long as she comes in for drips.'

Joyfully I collected her and made arrangements for taking her in for these necessary procedures. When we got there she would be set to lie in comfort on a table and attached to the drip while a chair was brought for me so that I could sit with her. A few minutes later, in sailed Irina with two steaming mugs – 'Coffee for the ladies!' One mug was for me, the other for Shari, and a small dish was provided for me to serve hers in. By the time the drip was all in, she would have had the whole mugful.

On one occasion, one of the nurses brought a minute hedgehog which she was hand rearing and fed it right under Shari's nose. Oh how thrilled she was. She had never seen such a thing before but I explained that it was a baby and that it was having its dinner. There is no doubt that she understood all this perfectly and didn't miss a minute of the performance. She was really happy and showed no nervousness of this strange room full of hospital equipment.

Once when they were a year or two old, we had a bad storm which brought down a tree across the back fence and Spangles took advantage of the gap to go for an unsupervised run. Black day! From the time that I lost my bad old Toffee, I had had no trouble with dogs running off but in Spangles I now found I had a runner and a long battle ensued in which I tried with very little success to stop her getting out again.

I put up a running line and chained her to it – completely useless. She would stand frozen in the exact pose in which she had been fastened up, a picture of cruelly used misery until I relented and let her off.

If there is one job I hate more than any other it is fencing, but I stuck grimly to it, composing a poem on my sufferings as I worked until I eventually got her corked up safely. But I couldn't let her go free at exercise or she would take off, so I compromised with a flexi lead, put on when the others were let loose. Spangles was a cheerful and generous dog and turned the knife in my heart by being overtly delighted whenever she saw me about to replace her short lead with this long one.

Shari was a great help when her pal went walkabout. I would tie three leads together and go hunting my missing dog in the orchards. I asked Shari where Spangles was. She always knew and, pulling on her long leash, would take me in the right direction. The strange thing was that Spangles would always come – or at least sit down and wait for me – once I caught sight of her. But not if I couldn't see her! Airedale mind-reading at its best!

On one occasion I recaptured her in this way and took her home, and a day or two later answered the door to the farm shepherd.

It was a man new to the job and he told me that he had been trying to find out where the Airedale came from that he had found in the sheep field recently.

He warned me to keep her in but said that he had not shot her because she was well away from the flock and trying to get through the fence to the person (me) whom he could hear calling for her.

In actual fact, odd as it may seem, I think Spangles was rather nervous of sheep. They were all a good bit bigger than she was and went about in large gangs, and it so happened that she had never got near enough to them to discover their tendency to bolt.

Unlike most of my dogs, Shari liked to lie in the bathroom. Probably she enjoyed the coolness of the floor tiles, and whenever I went in there to use the loo she would come with me. At these times, however, she had an ulterior motive, because she was obviously hoping that the toilet roll would run out and that she would be presented with the cardboard tube from the centre, a toy much prized by all the gang.

But Shari didn't just hope – she could measure the roll with an experienced eye. If it looked near the end, she would settle down to await the prize, but if it was still big and fat she would give up in disgust and walk off.

Why does this cardboard tube exercise such fascination over so many dogs? We all know the Andrex puppy advertisements. I can only say that Saffron in particular at one time seemed to have a life's ambition to cover my entire garden in pink loo paper and on several occasions very nearly succeeded.

Song Of Spangles

1. Our garden's great,
    It's wild and big,
    With rats to hunt
    And holes to dig,
    I've pals to chase
    (And that makes sense)
    But best of all
    There is – the fence!

2. When I was young,
    The world so wide
    Was lost on me –
    It was Outside,
    But one dark night
    A storm-hit tree
    Brought down the fence
    And I was free.

3. I found a land
    Of field and wood
    So wild and wide,
    So gay, so good,
    That joy of flight
    On legs so strong
    And feet so fleet
    Could not be wrong

4. But then my Mum
    Said 'Not again!'
    And tied me up
    With wire and chain.
    She mended fence
    Then called a truce,
    And with a kiss
    She turned me loose.

5. The fence was patched,
    Old wire, not new,
    It wasn't hard,
    I soon was through.
    She couldn't win,
    I was too quick,
    So her next move
    Was – send for Mick!

6. When Mick arrived
    With posts and link
    He built a fence
    As quick as wink.
    The fence was high,
    The fence was long –
    What could I do?
    It was so strong!

7. I squeezed beneath –
    All terrier dogs
    Will think of this –
    But then with logs
    And broken post
    And chunks of stone
    Mum barred my way
    And did she moan.

8. This would not do,
    It could not last,
    I pelted out,
    And running fast
    I jumped and caught
    The topmost wire –
    Jolly good job
    It was not higher.

9. Once more I danced
    About the farm,
    A happy dog
    Who did no harm,
    And if a duckpond
    Crossed my path
    Why did I need
    To have a bath?

10. With metal bars
    And chicken wire
    My Mum then made
    The fence still higher.
    She was surprised
    When I got through –
    I simply pushed
    Between the two.

11. Now every day
    She sews the gap
    With iron thread
    To close the trap.
    Her nose is red,
    Her lips are blue,
    She mutters words
    That match them too.

12. This lovely game
    Will have no end,
    I'll gallop just
    Where I intend,
    For when the fence
    Becomes too tall
    I'll learn to jump
    The garden wall.

13. To scale the gates
    Should not be hard,
    For I am such
    A knowing card.
    I love my Mum
    Who plays my game.
    I bet I beat her
    All the same!

18

Puppies Galore

We had come into the land of sweet content and these were in truth happy years. They were certainly full of very hard work for me, but I had plenty of trimming work, my bitches steadily produced two litters every year, puppy sales were good, and, besides keeping my head above water, I was able to spend a little money on the maintenance and improvement of my home. Every room was redecorated and some much-needed rewiring and replumbing was also done.

I somewhat ambitiously remodelled the kitchen with a scheme bought as flat-pack from a Do-It-Yourself store. My minivan was invaluable in getting all this gear home – I found just the worktop I wanted, fifteen feet long and very cheap. The only snag was that my proposed surface was only eleven feet and the store refused to cut it for me.

A shop assistant took pity on me and let me go to the warehouse and cut it myself with a borrowed saw, strictly against regulations – it seems so silly. When I had done this, he loaded it into my van (it weighed a ton) where it defied my best efforts to stow it in an acceptable manner.

At last I got it securely anchored with the aid of some spare dog leads so that the rear end which protruded from the back doors just cleared the ground. I drove home furtively through the back lanes and arrived in triumph with no further incident.

Getting it out of the van and into the house was not easy, but I managed it somehow with the aid of my little aluminium trolley, which in its time also shifted fridges, freezers and washing machines. Dot helped me to heave it up on to the cupboards which were to support it. One of the idiosyncrasies of my skill as a builder and decorator is that I am unable to measure things correctly and sure enough I found that I had cut it short by an inch and a half. Oh well, I thought, at least it will go in. Much worse if it had been too long. This worktop is still in place and looks as good now as when I first bought it.

It did come as rather a shock to find how heavy these flatpack items were. For a time I was at a loss to know how I was going to lift and fix the big double cupboard which I proposed to hang on the wall overhead. But all these problems can be resolved. First putting a layer of newspaper on the worktop, I brought in a number of loose bricks and laid them ready. Then, lifting up the carcass of the cupboard without doors or shelves (all I could shift) I put a brick under one end, then under the other and continued like this with a seesaw sort of action until the cupboard was at the right height. I then fixed it to the wall, added doors and shelves and removed the bricks.

Another big improvement to the kitchen was my new ceramic tile floor. I had tired of successive litters of pups tearing up my old vinyl. This new floor was never endangered that way and was blissfully easy to clean.

While on the subject of the liquid produce of my dogs, it amazes many people that my grass is green and unscarred by brown patches. Frankly I don't know the answer to this one. It can't just be one of the many advantages of the Airedale breed that they don't burn the grass because my Dandie and other breeds also lived here for several years and all was well. Nor can it be the soil because I have never had this trouble in any other garden either.

It could be the food – meat with a high proportion of tripe and wheat meal. Keeping to the old ways, I do not feed the fashionable dried foods. I don't doubt their nutritive values but I feel for the dogs. Would you like to live all your life on hard dried rations?

A dog doesn't have much in its life, only the pleasure of a good bed, its owner's kindness, the excitement of a walk and the wonderful joy of eating its dinner – why deprive him of this last privilege by replacing it with such uninteresting fare?

On one occasion I was advised to put one of my present dogs on to a leading brand. She loved it for the first two days, then showed some disappointment at meal times, and before the week was out was leaving it and trying to steal her daughter's portion instead. I put her back on to real food. After all, this is the natural way. Is a dog's digestion designed to cope solely with these unappetising pellets?

Puppy times were always happy although very busy. Luckily Christina was more than willing to help. Litter size varied a good deal, the largest being a family of thirteen produced by Spangles. Unfortunately they did not all survive.

Pup number eleven was born dead through no fault of either Spangles or myself. She gave birth rather tiredly by then but perfectly naturally, and I saw the expected solid little parcel slide onto the floor of the box and lie among its blood and broken membranes like all its ten siblings already produced. Its mum set about the usual cleaning-up job with energy and efficiency while I, leaving nothing to chance, snipped at the thick membrane covering the head and slid it back round the neck so that Number Eleven could take his first breath. But he didn't. Heavy and still he lay, a dead thing among the squirming swarm of life around him.

I couldn't believe it. I grabbed him and severed the cord, the better to be able to handle him roughly. I held him in a dry towel and rubbed him fiercely, expecting that first convulsive jerk and gasp. Nothing.

There was a fine line of milky foam round his lips. Fluid in the lungs? Remembering an old lesson from my vet, I began to swing him hard, head down, backwards and forwards. Nothing.

I tried the kiss of life and felt the tiny chest expand as the air went in. Nothing.

I remembered, from God knows where, that one can give artificial respiration to a newborn whelp by alternately stretching and doubling up the little body. This might expel the air I had blown in, and for two or three minutes – it seemed – I alternated this with the kiss of life.

The jaws gaped. I stared. Was this a real movement or, as it easily could have been, simply a result of my rough handling? I didn't know, but, frantic to intensify my efforts, I remembered the tiny bottle of brandy I keep in my puppy kit for such emergencies. But I hadn't used it for years – was it still there? I scrabbled frantically, despairingly, among the box's contents, nearly tipping the lot on the floor because I could only spare one hand for the job. The other was still massaging the little corpse.

At last! There was the bottle, underneath everything else. I got it out together with a small syringe and unscrewed the minute cap one-handed. Damn, there was nothing to pour the brandy into and the syringe wouldn't go into the bottle. Somehow I managed to tip a little into the cap, spilling some in the process and more in trying to find a flat space big enough to stand the lidless bottle on.

Should be half water but no time for that, he'll have to have it neat. Damn again. The syringe, dry from disuse, wouldn't pull, and I couldn't draw any brandy into it. Only one thing to do, use it as a dipstick and drop one, two, three drops on his tongue. The vapour should be enough.

And it was. Slowly, weakly, my little corpse was coming to life. Hardly believing my eyes, I put him to Spangles's nipple but he hadn't enough strength to grasp it. Three times I squeezed milky drops out and put his mouth over it. The third time, he began to suck and, believe it or not, in half an hour I couldn't pick him out from the rest of the gang.

That was the event of the week for me, because in that frantic struggle at the dawning of his life, I was, for him, God.

These thirteen puppies looked so beautiful they gave me a real thrill. I once found them laid in a long straight line diagonally from corner to corner of the box like a string of beads, all identical. But to my sorrow they soon began to succumb to a mysterious illness.

The vet put them on Penbritin, which was then new to veterinary science and still came in liquid form. They continued to die. One poor little bitch was so poorly that she cried continually with a thin high wail unbearable to hear. At last I wrapped her in a scrap of towelling and took her to bed with me. She stopped crying, seemed comforted and slept all night in the warm in the hollow of my shoulder – but in the morning she too died.

In desperation, I read the (very) small print on the leaflet which had come with the Penbritin and learned that the dose could be doubled in intransigent cases. Feeling I had nothing to lose, I did this and could hardly believe it when my invalids began to recover. I lost no more and finished with seven of the original bakers' dozen.

These puppies seemed none the worse afterwards, grew well and lived long healthy lives. I never did find out what had ailed them, a small tragedy as the world goes, but one I have never forgotten.

Parting with the puppies was an anxious time as I was determined that each should go to a good home and be a blessing to its owner. With supply so erratic – having any number from zero to sixteen available – customers often had to wait months until some pups had reached the magic age of six to twelve weeks when it was the best time to move them to a new home.

Each owner would receive a pedigree, a sheet of feeding instructions, information on vaccinations needed and much else besides. Even then, an occasional pup would be returned, for a variety of reasons, but like all good breeders I would always take back one of my own Caterways line and find a new home for it, even if a year or two old.

It is always heartening to find that the customer has given some thought to the practicalities and responsibilities of keeping a pet, for truly 'A dog is for life, not just for Christmas'. There is one such customer, however, I will never forget. He came for one of The Sixteen after seeing their photograph in the local paper.

The gentleman in question had previously had an Airedale from a well-known kennel, although he would not tell me which one. This dog had been well loved but was pitifully nervous. This time he meant to make no mistakes. Apparently he had seen and rejected two or three other litters before seeing mine, and then I think he was impressed because they were careering unchecked around the garden like a herd of small deer, also by the manner in which the three adults greeted him with wagging tails and inquisitive sniffings. With muddy paws too, but he didn't mind that, a sure point in his favour.

What really imprinted him on my memory was his reaction to my answer when he asked the price. I had two prices – a basic one and one a few pounds higher which I was asking for several puppies which showed promise of being handsomer breed specimens than the others.

He picked one of these and when I pointed out that it was one of the more expensive ones he replied that, since he expected the dog to cost well over a thousand pounds during its lifetime, it would be a poor economy to begrudge an extra few pounds at the start for an animal which would give him that much more pleasure to look at for all that time.

He had worked it out on a life expectancy of ten years, two pounds a week for food plus inoculations, vets' fees, boarding kennels, trimming, even to bedding, collars and leads.

It was a perfectly sensible way of looking at it but I admit to being a trifle staggered! This was a long time ago. If everyone thought like that today, I wonder if they too would opt for the more expensive and hopefully more beautiful dog, or if they would give up the whole idea and get a gerbil instead!

It is years now since my elderly bitches produced any litters and I think back on those days of puppies galore with great pleasure. I think I liked them best from three weeks of age, when they first became little dogs, to six weeks. They would begin exploring the garden and discovering themselves too, and exhibiting the beginnings of true Airedale pride and self confidence.

You could say of each that here was a pup that thought something of himself! I miss them very much. The old puppy shed is a bleak and dreary place without them and the hollows and hidey-holes around the garden are so pathetically empty with no little black and tan adventurers to explore them.

My hands remember the feel of those firm and warm little bodies that squirmed in ecstasy when I picked them up for a cuddle. My last puppies are many years old now but I'm still suffering from withdrawal symptoms, not helped by the fact that seldom does a week pass without someone phoning to ask if I have any for sale.

19
Help At Last

For years I grumbled that no one helps a single woman who is neither young nor pretty. The occasional help I have received has been almost always from a woman, or a husband volunteered by his wife. As a result, I have come to rely on myself to do all the gardening, cleaning, mowing, carpentry, concreting, mending windows, dressmaking, paperhanging, painting, washing the car, breeding puppies and grooming dogs.

I have thoroughly enjoyed it but anno domini catches up with us all and there were certainly times when I wished for an assistant, preferably both servile and silent.

But suddenly all that changed. The root cause was Val. Val wanted one of my puppies so badly that, to use the modern idiom, she could taste it. In fact, she had wanted one for years. She liked to ease her fever by seeing a lot of my pack of five, and since she is a talented and lovely person she was always welcome.

One day she arrived with a surprise present I couldn't refuse, although following an impoverished childhood I normally neither give nor accept spontaneous gifts. It was a circular ceramic plaque with the head of an Airedale painted on it. She had both made and painted it herself.

Where did I want it? I chose a spot halfway between the side window and the back door, at the time occupied by a rickety, home-made wall.

I explained that I intended to demolish this before it fell down, and was thinking of replacing it with brick posts and a proper gate.

Oh dear, that did it. Val came back, dug three holes and started laying concrete foundation for the posts. I bought a stiff wire panel at great expense to edge the path and began shopping around for bricks. Val firmly told me to leave it to her. She canvassed her extensive family and phoned to tell me the bricks were being delivered and I mustn't touch them. She had roped in a brother-in-law to do the job for her.

Mo, the brother-in-law, arrived one day soon after eight while I was washing the kitchen floor. Naturally, it was the day I expected two Old English sheepdogs – new customers – for clipping. They duly arrived and were steered somewhat perilously between a pile of wet cement and the emerging gateposts.

One of the sheepdogs made a quite unexpected grab at Christina's face but luckily was on a short lead and I just jerked it clear. Christina had a near escape from losing a good deal of skin and probably some features too. Val meantime had arrived and retired to the end of the garden where she was clearing a patch of jungle grown through old wire fencing thrown down years ago.

Lyn, the young lady from the council, came to check the purity of my spring water. She is very nice and keeps goats but today she brought a young man who was to succeed her. I was sorry and she said she would miss the Airedales who always gave her an enthusiastic welcome.

The sheepdogs were collected and Val and I made a scratch meal for the four of us. Mo was also hoping for one of my next lot of puppies and wouldn't hear of my paying him. This was a relief as I couldn't afford the luxury of professional bricklaying and would rather have built the posts myself.

I began to feel rather overwhelmed. The two gateposts, startlingly upright, were growing steadily on either side of the path. I missed my post-prandial ten minutes' shut-eye, felt sleepy and longed to sit down, but felt obliged to show willing by going up the garden and helping Val.

Under her energetic attack, my garden had suddenly grown a new area but the ground was still woefully fouled with wire, glass, rotting posts, rope and old broken bricks. She was stamping manfully on rolls of tattered fencing in an endeavour to compress it into minivan-sized bundles. I got my bowsaw and wire snips and began extracting posts and saving them up so I could get rid of them on the house fire. The bonfire which I had only just reduced to a small mound of ashes was once more obliterated beneath a tepee of leaves and green branches. Oh dear.

Christina was coming down with a heavy cold. Val, who is childless, had adopted her as a surrogate daughter and dosed her at regular intervals with Beecham's powders and vitamin C. I saw the funny side of this and reminded Christina that she had a real mother who would probably do the same when she returned home. She looked mutinous but tossed back her medicine with gasps and groans.

Three o'clock. Christina fed the dogs and washed up while I struggled feebly to keep up with Val. Mo finished his twin posts and said he would be back in a fortnight. A fortnight without a side gate!

I bid my friends goodbye and promised to use Mo's surplus blob of wet cement. Christina and Peanut got into Val's car and were borne homeward. Mo put his gear into his car and went too. I went indoors, switched on the telly and collapsed. But the fading light reminded me of the wet cement and I dragged myself out to scoop it up and bung it into the foundations.

Indoors once more, I decided to change early for bed but the dogs barked, and there in the failing light was Christina with Philip her boyfriend. She looked glamorous indeed but underdressed for the cooling day and sounded adenoidal.

She had brought Philip about some trees I wanted cut, but he had only come to look them over, not to do the job there and then.

Thank goodness! I had really had as much help as I could take for one day.

With work increasing, I had decided to take on a YTS trainee. Not being one of Nature's employers, I am embarrassed to ask people to spend time and energy for the meagre rewards I can afford. However in Christina's case there was little hesitation. Here was a girl with no other prospects, who ardently wished to work with dogs. I knew I could give her a good training and she would receive not only modest earnings but a regular sum from the State.

There were other considerations. Christina, who was born nearby, regarded me as a favourite auntie and spent much of her time here for the love of me and my dogs. Invariably arriving uninvited, it never occurred to her that she might be unwelcome. Robbed of my solitude, interrupted in my work, I have somehow concealed my annoyance but found her presence extremely tiring.

Christina was now a good-looking girl, tall and slim with shining blonde hair, clear blue eyes and a beautiful skin. She had a happy enthusiasm for just about everything and a devastating abundance of conversation. How she could talk! As a devout loner, could I stand company five days a week?

A trainee however, would be in a different category from an uninvited visitor. I would know when to expect her and would be entitled to make her work and curb her excesses. On the whole I thought I would be doing her a good turn so I made my proposition. It would be hard to describe the joy with which it was received.

We had a few problems but they have been very small. Christina was boundlessly energetic but biddable. The dogs loved her and she has a genuine flair for handling them. Her training came on by leaps and bounds in spite of a slight contretemps when a visiting spaniel snapped at the scissors, cutting his tongue.

This little accident shattered her for several days. It was beneficial in curbing her growing over-confidence, but she took some time to regain the courage to use the scissors when necessary. However her hand stripping is really wonderful, and as this is quite a rare talent as well as being very hard work, I felt we were both lucky.

As well as getting on famously with the dogs, she was popular with my customers, many of whom stay on to watch their dogs trimmed. I think this daily contact with the public, most of whom are very nice indeed, remedied any deficiency in her being restricted to one workmate, myself.

The job was not only trimming: general kennel work provided a welcome change. This was mostly dishing out the dogs' dinners and putting them in the oven to defrost by three o'clock. She also cleaned the grass of dog dirt every day.

Her most spectacular task was reviving a tiny pup who became separated from the litter one cold November day. He was so cold that he was stiff and showing little sign of life. I gave him brandy and water and then handed him to Christina to mother while I stripped a customer's Scottie. I hoped she would not be too distressed by his death so soon in her novitiate.

'Is he gone?' I asked anxiously when the Scottie was done. A bright look met me. 'Gone? No, he's not – he's in there fighting like a good 'un,' she said, pointing to the mother and her complete litter noisily suckling. He would certainly have died but for her. Her delight was a joy to see and I was then sure that my trainee was a square peg in a good square hole.

When Christina finished her YTS year she still worked with me, but was self-employed. I gave her three quarters of the money she earned and a pound a day as a token for other duties.

Because she was 'self-employed', I very rarely asked her to do anything beyond preparing the dogs' dinners, and, believe me, she even more rarely offered. Thus every day I prepared her lunch, handed it to her and washed up after her. On the days I went out in the afternoon, I knew the lunch dishes would be in the washing-up bowl on my return and the dogs' dishes stacked, still dirty, on the drainer.

In those far-off days before I became an employer, I used to look askance at those kennel owners who spoke with one voice about the irritation value and general uselessness of their assistants. A little more tolerance, I felt, and all this could be avoided. Besides, when I took the plunge I chose carefully a girl known intimately from babyhood who regarded me and my dogs as an extension of her family.

My feelings towards her did change somewhat when, deaf to my protestations, she acquired Astra, an Alsatian. You may think it was no business of mine what dog she had, but she assumed as a matter of course that she would bring Astra to work every day.

The Alsatian was ornamental and played patiently with my current pup, but was very irritating to have around. She crashed through everything in the garden like a tank, and met my poor customers with gnashing teeth, ferocious snarls and a coat raised like a hedgehog.

She was hyperactive and enjoyed carrying my logs around the garden, a trick that greatly amused Christina. It never occurred to her to collect them at the end of the day so that I didn't have to rake under trees to rebuild my woodpile.

Altogether I was surprisingly thrilled to have a four week holiday over Christmas with no assistant.

20
Making A Dog Garden

With so much wheel-barrowing of heavy loads, an early requirement was a path running the length of the garden. As I like things to look reasonably decorative, my path followed the natural curve taken by my feet and the paws of the dogs from the house to the big shed. I began by laying down my spare stone slabs, spaced more or less evenly, and collecting the bricks which lay scattered among the grass and weeds. These were used as infilling between the slabs, arranged in patterns of red and white like parquet.

Like the drive, this path (soon christened the M1) was laid flush with the ground for easy mowing. The bricks turned up in seemingly inexhaustible numbers and were more than enough to cover the distance. It still gives me pleasure to walk over it.

When the drive was bulldozed out of the front bank, the spoil was spread over a low-lying corner of the garden creating a skidpan of sticky clay which needed to be grassed over. I levelled it and cleaned it, but having no money for turves, resorted to a method I had used before with success.

As summer arrived, up came the weeds. I mowed these regularly, killing any nettles and other tall invaders, and in a few months was mowing grass. In Kent, grass grows as easily as the rain falls. Nature laid my grass for me at no expense and with a minimum of fuss and soon I had a new dog paddock. It is certainly a method to recommend to anyone with a lot of ground to cover.

All this sounds as if I were some sort of Amazon, but alas I am not and never have been. Most of my life I have been handicapped by thyroid deficiency which makes the sufferer stout and lazy, and although I did not know it at the time, I was being badly overdosed with thyroxine. This meant that I was plagued by palpitations, an absolutely infuriating complaint as it is so disabling.

In those early years, whole summers went by when I was able to do no more than mark time and performed my dog trimming work with great difficulty, spurred on solely by the need to make ends meet. It was not until I had a new doctor, who at once reduced my dosage, that my health improved.

I often browse through the fascinating articles in gardening magazines but have never come across one featuring my own dilemma. Yet surely there are many readers facing the same problems of successfully integrating an interesting garden with energetic dogs.

All my life I have pursued both hobbies and have painfully learned various stratagems to reduce mutual damage. Never were these more necessary than when I kept five Airedales and a Dandie and was breeding two or three litters a year, as well as welcoming visiting dogs. Yes, you may say I had problems.

My garden is a good one for dogs, nearly a fifth of an acre with interest on all sides so that they keep busy. It soon became obvious where they were running, and it was on their tracks that I laid my paths. A wide stretch of mosaic paving inside the drive fence not only greatly reduced the mud brought into the house but tightened up their feet beautifully.

Many years ago I was somewhat bemused by a neighbour whose first act on taking over his large and rough garden was to lay a twelve inch concrete path right round it just inside the fence. He explained that his Alsatian had a habit of constantly patrolling his fences. By providing a hard track for this, he was taking a sensible precaution.

He planned his garden inside this perimeter. With the growth of his shrubs and trees the path quickly became invisible and no one knew it was there – except the Alsatian, who used it continually and never set paw on any of the beds.

Not everyone would have the room – or the need – for this. In past gardens, I stopped dogs rushing over flowerbeds to bark at cats and so on by building foot-high wire fences at right angles to the fence. These were soon covered by flowering plants and kept the dogs to the path. I do recommend anyone acquiring a puppy to build wire fences round especially loved plants and trees for the first years, after which they will probably be safe.

All my flowerbeds were planned outside my stout dog-proof fencing, so were around the house and either side of the drive. This gives me quite a lot of scope with mixed flowerbeds, rockery alpines by the drive and space for a buddleia.

There is also my very best plant – a gorgeous wisteria planted many years ago which now embraces a forty foot stretch of fence and is beautiful in all seasons. This blooms generously twice a year and is divinely scented.

This is really a spring garden, when bulbs, alpines and wallflowers are enough to make any gardener conceited. But alas, the end of May comes and the illuminations are dimmed. I am too busy in summer to follow up these pyrotechnics and the weeds return.

An excitement one year was the appearance of a sport from a packet of alyssum I sowed at the front. It was large, white and handsome and monitored by Thompson and Morgan to see whether it could be developed as a new variety. Alas, it was sterile and never set seed in its empty pods.

Most of the land is in the back garden, where the dogs have free run. Here I have to rely on paving, grass, shrubs and trees. At the back is a strip of scruffy 'woodland' through which I laid a row of paving stones as it is a favourite playground for the gang.

Bluebells and hostas have been optimistically planted but little flourishes except ivy and Queen Anne's lace.

There is a large shed in one corner used for puppies, with a generous run behind it. Here I grow cultivated blackberries to provide a welcome crop and to deter intruders who might think of taking my babies.

I planned two shrubberies to cross the garden as screens. Woman proposes and in this case a pack of dogs disposes. The trees on the whole did quite well considering their minuscule size on arrival. A weeping willow wand plucked from a customer's drive grew enthusiastically far taller than the cottage and provided a cool green tunnel of shade all summer.

I wanted an elegant silver birch and Tom kindly offered to dig one from the woods for me. I also bought a crab apple, a berberis and a red may tree. The best buy was a Woolworths amelanchier planted where I could see it from the kitchen window. Every spring throws a snowy lace curtain over this graceful tree, to be followed first by tiny dark cherries and then by colourful autumnal foliage.

A beech hedge planned to stand between the wire front fence and the top of the bank got off to a rocky start as only six of thirty-six rooted cuttings survived. Luckily they were evenly spaced and have become a handsome copper screen.

Gardening does tend to be a war of attrition between me and the dogs. All my shrubs were sedulously staked, however tiny, but lived precariously. The rear shrubbery was doomed by the close proximity of the wood and the voracious appetite for blossom bud displayed by the gangs of bird hoodlums who should have been decimating the insect population instead.

The front shrubbery had more room and light but less defence against the flying feet of exhilarated Airedales and the busy little teeth of puppies. Many were simply broken off at ground level.

I have already mentioned The Hole under the birch tree. Successive generations have spent blissful hours working on this. Sometimes it has as many as three entrances, then the whole thing collapses and they have to start all over again. Airedales, being terriers, are fond of digging, but mine generally confine it to The Hole despite the attractions of moles, mice, rats and rabbits to catch.

Occasionally I ploughed back some of my puppy money into the garden. My white aluminium furniture is dog-proof and looks nice in all weathers. Recently I erected a greenhouse beside the puppy shed, its glass walls protected by wire panels to fend off crash landings.

Damage in a garden is not all one-way. I wish garden advice sometimes stretched to considering the resident dog. Slug bait is too dangerous to use and I only apply weedkiller when the dogs are shut in until it has dried. Even then I worry: dogs love to eat couch grass in the spring – will dried weedkiller affect them?

Puppies can die from eating red-hot poker leaves or delphiniums, and foxgloves are too poisonous to plant in my little wood. I have learnt the hard way to dig up any plant that proves too attractive to wasps and bees. One sting in the throat can soon kill a dog. For the same reason, I have restricted fruit trees to one sprawling Bramley apple, and even then have to check under it regularly in summer to remove rotting fruit.

It is not difficult to teach one or two dogs to respect a garden but if it is to be a playground for a pack, with lively litters arriving regularly, you must accept that casualties are going to be high. Apply your intelligence and try to outwit the dog. Most kennel owners have given up the struggle and just keep the place tidy, but I still hanker after colour and flowers and I expect I shall still be optimistically planting shrubs when I'm ninety.

21
Babe In The Wood

It was thanks to Spangles's lust for the wide open spaces that Clarisse and I embarked on a strange experience. A careless customer came in one day and left the side gate open. Never slow to seize an opportunity, Spangles got out, melting into the fields and woods and sparking off a frantic search by ourselves, the offending customer and, it seemed at times, the entire village.

Leaping into our respective cars in order to extend our range, Clarisse and I went off in different directions. She went up the hill and into the woods.

In those days this district was invaded annually by troops of temporary workers, mostly gypsies or Londoners, come for the fruit picking. That year there had been a sizeable contingent of strange ragged scarecrows driving a collection of cars and vans so patched and feeble that, seeing them gasping and struggling to take on our little hills, one could only be amazed that the police had allowed them on the road from wherever they had come.

For months they were camped among the trees where Clarisse was headed, a shabby and slightly sinister eyesore in the pretty greenwood. With the onset of winter, most had melted away, but four or five vehicles obstinately persisted, slowly sinking into the damp leafmould, an offence and a reproach to the tidy-minded villagers.

Now gypsies have a great way with animals, and it occurred to Clarisse that they would find it simple to corral our truant and have her away for sale or whatever other nefarious purposes might occur to them.

Dog fighting, although illegal, is by no means unknown in Kent, and even unaggressive animals like Spangles might be used in training as bait. It would be better, she thought, to enlist their co-operation and suggest that we would be prepared to pay a reward for the safe return of our property. It was with some courage, I feel, that she pulled in to their camp and got out of the car to confront them.

As she did so, three or four young men appeared. They were young, bearded, some with short stubby dreadlocks, all unkempt and as ragged as the tramps in an old comic, even to the flapping toecaps.

But to her surprise, they showed real concern for the missing dog, which they earnestly assured her they would bring home should they find her. Not gypsies or hippies. Simple dropouts perhaps? We discovered later that they belonged to that sad classless society known now as New Age Travellers.

There was a young woman chopping wood among the trees, and she too came forward to join the talk. 'Would you like a cup of tea?' she asked. 'In your van?' said Clarisse, somewhat taken aback. 'In my bender' replied the girl, 'I haven't got a van.'

Clarisse had no idea what a bender might be, but followed trustingly further into the wood. What she saw brought her up short, for what the girl had was really nothing but a wigwam. Slim saplings had been bent towards each other and fastened together – hence the name, no doubt.

A thick layer of polythene, carpet, etc. made the roof and walls, while the floor was grubby carpet, several layers by the feel of it, laid over wooden pallets to keep it off the ground. There was a tiny stove in one corner with the chimney poking through the skin of the bender. Pam – that was the girl's name – said that they had been shown how to make benders by gypsies at Greenham Common.

All this was sufficiently surprising to Clarisse but the bender held yet another item which fairly rocked her to her foundations. It was a tiny baby, a little boy only four months old and named Cassius. He was spotlessly clean and as warm as toast in his primitive nursery, and when Pam changed his nappy she revealed a smooth pink bottom free of any soreness or rash.

Clarisse told me all this with a dazed expression on her face when we met again (our truant strolled in again at dusk).

Pam had run away from a drunken father and a hellfire Catholic mother. Welfare services had given her a room in Maidstone but she had found it insupportable, the landlord being a bully and a rogue. She still used it as an accommodation address for the purpose of getting her state allowances, so was not actually destitute.

There's a lot of the social worker in Clarisse. She went back next day bearing food and disposable nappies, and later we went together as I was anxious to see these strange birds of passage.

And I confess we did find them strange. The men would go, in whichever vehicle would move, to London, there hopefully to earn money busking to theatre queues. They would also undertake any local work which offered, but with fruit picking now no more than a memory this was practically non-existent.

We saw no other women but all the group seemed to care for each other and Cassius was handed in to one of their vans whenever Pam had to leave him. He was warm and well-cared for but seemed very small to me for four months, and we felt this was in part due to the fact that they were all vegetarian so that he was getting no protein apart from the milk, both human and powdered, which was still his sole diet.

The weather that week was bitterly cold. Clarisse cooked a huge vegetable stew which was greeted with delight by all the group when we took it to them. They all looked very thin and hungry, but were gentle, soft spoken folk. We did put ourselves out to give them some help and this was received gratefully without resentment or loss of dignity in the same spirit as it was offered.

I phoned a friend who lived in a constant state of organising jumble sales for the Guide Dogs and she gave me a huge bundle of baby things from shawls right down to rattles. Pam was over the moon with these, for as she said, drying clean clothes was a constant problem. We took her any canned vegetables we had, candles and knitting wool, for she had begun to knit for her baby.

I offered a little work pruning my garden. Dave (they all seemed to be called Dave) jumped at it eagerly and came flapping down the hill in his monstrous footwear to cut hedges and trim trees. He worked hard and, on being rewarded with a cup of coffee, toasted cheese and a tenner, flapped away in high spirits in search of the village and more food.

A few evenings later I was sitting alone, Clarisse being away for a couple of days, when there was a knock at the front door. As it was nearly ten o'clock, my first thought was that it was Clarisse returned unexpectedly, but to my surprise it was Pam.

On asking her in I saw that she was very distressed, white, shaking and very thin. She apologised for disturbing me at that hour but said that she had nowhere else to turn for help and reminded me that I had told her to come if she were in trouble.

And she was – her bender had burnt to the ground and she had lost all her few possessions. Naturally my first thought was for Cassius but true to form she had taken him with her as she was drinking coffee in a friend's van.

But she had lost her bed, the baby's carrycot which was also his cradle, all her spare clothes, her allowance book, the beautiful bundle of baby things from the jumble sale – in fact everything except the things she and Cassius were wearing at the time.

I felt helpless. The shops were all shut and most of my few spare things had already been passed on to her. She asked if I had any old sheeting which she could tear up to make nappies for Cassius, and after making her a cup of coffee I went upstairs to reconnoitre. She had been told she could sleep in another camper's van but she had no bedding. Luckily I found a couple of spare blankets, two pillows and a small knitted coverlet. For want of pillowslips, I used two large cushion covers also destined for the jumble sale.

There was little food in the house. I managed to produce two pints of milk but Cassius's food was still a worry. Pam said she was trying to feed him herself, but it only took one look at her thin frame to see that this was not an option which gave him much hope.

Looking through my depleted store cupboard, I did find an unopened packet of Casilan – bought for Samba's puppies and unused. Rather desperately I offered this to Pam, admitting why I had bought it but suggesting that it might bridge the gap for the baby until his usual milk powder could be purchased.

Pam looked a little frightened, saying that dogs and people were different. 'Not much when they are very young,' I said firmly. 'Their needs are really very similar at that stage, and in any case this is not a dog food, it's a food made for people and it's a very good one and very pure.'

She took the box and some glucose and I wrote out the formula which I used for feeding newborn puppies, only recommending that she diluted it a little for the baby. I will say here that a few days later she told me eagerly that it had saved the day. Cassius had taken it with enthusiasm, had been contented afterwards and had suffered no ill effects of any kind. I hope she finished the packet herself. She looked as if she needed it.

People started to warn Clarisse and myself that we were being imposed upon but neither of us ever felt that. Next morning I went shopping and bought Pam a sort of survival kit from supermarket and chemist and took it to her. She invited me into Dave's van where Cassius was lying on my old pillows, wrapped in my tattered blankets. He was wearing nothing but a nappy and rubber pants.

He was lovely, as fair as could be and so happy – I never saw a happier baby. He threw the blankets off and when I placed my hand under his feet he kicked against it and chuckled and blew bubbles.

His sole surviving suit had been washed and was drying on a string stretched across the van.

Pam wrapped him up and took me to see the damage. No deception there, the bender was nothing but a black circle of ash with little recognisable except the mattress springs and the twisted skeleton of the carrycot.

Pam thought the candle left burning against her return had fallen over but another camper told Clarisse that it was more likely arson, judging from the fierceness of the blaze.

Pam had been proud of her bender and said to me pathetically that she had made it so good it was the nicest place she had ever lived in.
No good going back to the jumble sale. We had cleaned it out. However Joe, the baby's father, came back from town and Pam sent him into Maidstone with a little money to buy Cassius some clothes.
Not knowing what to get, he went into a big baby clothes shop, told the assistant what had happened and asked her advice. She disappeared into the back of the shop, reappearing after an interval with the manageress and a big parcel of things which they gave him.

Meanwhile Clarisse, ever resourceful, had rung a friend, the owner of two toddlers, and produced a huge bounty of all possible things needed, so the young woodsman was once again provided for.

Joe announced his intention to stay in Kent and set to work on a new bender. Clarisse took him aside and gave him a lecture on looking after his baby and its mother. She told him what a good girl we thought Pam was to make such a good job of caring for this tiny creature under almost impossible conditions, and thought she made some impression.

Joe took his lecture in the spirit in which it was offered and showed no resentment of Clarisse's interest in his affairs. Clarisse also went to the wood alone one evening on a purely social visit, drank tea with them at their camp fire and talked at length with Rastafarian Dave, a half-caste who claimed to be a healer and offered to heal her injured leg which that evening was very painful. He rubbed it with what he said was tiger balm. Alas, it didn't work.

Before the fire, Pam had given each of us a small bracelet made of braided threads of many colours which she had made herself. She had a collection of these friendship bands and sold them as lucky charms, but it perished in the blaze along with all her other possessions.

I still have my bracelet and think of poor Pam whenever I come across it. These things were all she could give us to express her gratitude for our help.

I bought her some little tins and jars of food for weaning babies. They were quite new to her. She was amazed at Cassius's enthusiasm for them, and Clarisse was able to teach her some useful rules for advancing his feeding regime. I really don't know what she would have done without this information as she seemed to have no previous experience, either her own or friends' or relatives', to go on.

Nearer Christmas, Clarisse baked them a big Christmas cake and we took them a present of food and a teddy for Cassius. We did try to get the men some trousers and footwear. One tall thin lad named Tadpole had size thirteen feet, and since these need shoes made specially for them at a price of over two hundred pounds, I can't imagine how he ever found anything at all. I believe his mother used to send him the occasional pair of plimsolls. Pam, incidentally, would never accept any money from us although I once got her to take a present in that form for Cassius.

Clarisse, whose initiative frequently left me gasping, even persuaded a man working behind a supermarket store to give her two wooden pallets, including loading them into her car. These were to replace some of those burnt beneath the floor of the original bender.

The reactions of friends to this situation fascinated us with their wild variations. We never felt uncomfortable about it or had any feeling that we were being taken advantage of. Most of what we gave was stuff we did not want, or which had been given us to pass on.

Although we both spent money buying various things (mostly food) for them, we did not give to the advertised charities that year so we gave nothing which we couldn't afford. And in that bleak winter season, it was impossible not to think of another baby who came into a bare and hostile world.

The campers' nearest neighbour was an old customer of mine who told me later that she had nothing against them as they were quiet and well behaved. They did make the pretty woodland look untidy, not least because they had a permanent heap of old iron which they collected to sell for a few pounds. Eventually the council moved them on and we lost touch.

The last I heard of them was that Pam was very excited because Joe was trying to buy a large van of the sort which has an extension, a sort of upper storey, above the driver's cabin. She was planning to use this as a bedroom which would be separate from their daytime living space. I hope she got it.

We may think it an obscenity that, in a wealthy and highly organised society, people should be forced to live like this, or we may blame the irresponsibility and stubborness of those who will get themselves into such a situation. For myself I'm not much interested in how it happened. I can easily imagine myself in their shoes, holes and all, but I can't easily imagine a satisfactory and practical way out for any of them. In the end it must be up to them.

And as for Cassius, the babe in the wood, he kicked and gurgled and blew bubbles to his young mother's white face. No amount of imagination at all could make it his fault. Let us hope the world will deal more kindly with him than it did with his parents.

22
Hurricane

Dot and Nobby left their jobs on the farm and to my sorrow had to leave their tied cottage and move into the main village, thus depriving me of the best neighbours I have ever had. I still saw plenty of Christina, of course. The loss of Dot made Clarisse's presence all the more welcome to me especially as we both have the same approach to dogs and the way they should be kept.

For me she was a lot of fun. For her it was an opportunity to relax, take stock and get the tumult of her private life back into some semblance of order. But she did feel that she should be taking charge of her own fortunes, and for this reason she left me and went down to stay with her father on the coast with the idea of qualifying for some line of work which should provide her with a career.

So it was that she was not living here one day when I picked Tina and Astra up and, with an assortment of my own dogs, drove to our training club, nearly an hour away.

I remember being much impressed by the appearance of the sky, which was like no other I had ever seen. It was very windy and it was only Tina's eagerness to work Astra in the third class which stopped me heading for home as soon as I had taken the first one. There was obviously going to be a storm and torrential rain might give us some trouble with flooded roads.

However we got away at last and absolutely tore home, splashing over dark roads and hurtling helter-skelter beneath tossing branches.

Scudding through the dark lanes, the mini seemed to be blown along by the ever-strengthening wind. I dropped Tina at her gate in the village, only remarking that we had been lucky to reach home so quickly, got home thankfully, settled the dogs and went to bed.

It was certainly a trip I would not have made had the weathermen been up to their job!

I fell into bed and into my usual deep sleep. It is so quiet here at night that, once having dived under the bedclothes in the velvet dark, it takes a lot to wake me. But this night was different. It may have been the willow cracking which woke me as, even before I heard the wind, I was aware of some large object being thrown across my window. The sky was so light I thought dawn was breaking, but then I saw the flicker of distant lightning all around – only it wasn't lightning.

I discovered later that it was the flashes of electric cables being torn down for miles around. The thrown object proved to be nothing but masses of willow tresses flying madly about then dropping back into place only to be thrown again.

It was half past four. No electricity. Hardly surprising as our overhead supply is not infrequently interrupted by bad weather. The racket was so bad that I became nervous of being upstairs in case the chimney stack blew down on top of me. So finding my slippers in the dark, I went downstairs, picking up the torch which I always keep on the bottom stair.

The dogs were pleased to see me but didn't seem unduly worried. They rushed to the back door as they usually do first thing in the morning, ready to run out as soon as it was open. But they were greeted by such a howling gale that, with a screech of brakes, one and all changed their minds and retreated promptly to the kitchen.

Luckily I had three boxes of candles from way back, so lighting my small Calor gas fire, I dressed and settled in my chair with a blanket, book and candle trying to ignore the uproar. Unsuccessfully, but at last it began to be daylight and the wind ever so slightly began to abate.

At half past seven the dogs jumped up and barked. When I opened the back door, I discovered that the drainpipe which takes all the water from the whole roof had been wrenched off the wall and gone through the conservatory roof. This roof is of polyurethane and the wind thus admitted proceeded to remove half of it. Thus all the rain from the housetop – and it was now pouring Niagaras – shot into this small space which rapidly became a pond.

Now the appalling noise of the storm began to have a numbing effect on my brain. Why else did I try to keep the power point dry by wrapping it in plastic and newspaper? Then by slipping a piece of cardboard under the lead flashing as a mini roof? It was hours before I realised that a square rubber car mat would do the job much better.

This was no time to be alone and, of course, I wanted help. At eight o'clock I wrote a note to Robin, the village builder, asking him to come. No phone of course, and this was something which had never failed before.

I went along to a neighbour whose husband was the farm manager, and saw that the lane was blocked by two fallen trees. Barbara was getting her children ready for school and agreed to deliver my note.

Coming back I saw that men were already working on the fallen trees. In the event, Barbara only got as far as the outskirts of the village. She learned that the school was closed and turned back after passing my note to a villager who promised to deliver it. But it was soon evident to me that assistance would be a long time coming.

Christina arrived for work with tales of houses with holes in their roofs and a situation of chaos obviously not soon to be resolved. We had eighty pounds worth of trimming booked in for that day and the next, but it was obvious that no one would arrive.

As the wind dropped, we spent most of the day sawing the trunk of the hawthorn tree which had fallen across the garden path. We got its big mophead of branches off, leaving about six feet of trunk leaning across the path. We could now weave our way between the two.

I went across the road to the Manor to tell Mr. Prance, who also owned the wood alongside my garden, that some of his trees had fallen on my fence. He soon came across and cut their tops off, relieving the pressure and my mind in one go. I had invested in some five foot chain link with concrete posts some years earlier, and how I blessed its sturdy victory over this terrible trial of its strength. Definitely one of my better buys.

I let Tina go early and attempted to drive her home. The nearby trees had been cleared but the corner leading to the village was completely stopped by a huge fallen poplar. Men with chainsaws were already hard at work on this, so Tina and Astra climbed across it and I backed the mini away.

An hour and a half later I tried again and was able to reach the village, where I bought a new battery for my torch and changed my Calor cylinder – a wise move as all these items were soon sold right out.

Back home, there seemed no prospect of hot food or drink. It was mid-October, not particularly cold but not warm either, and under these circumstances, pretty cheerless. I poured a cupful of water into a saucepan and balanced it on the Calor fire where it heated sufficiently to make a warm cup of coffee.

Luckily my coal bunker was well provisioned. How comforting a coal fire was, a balm to my beleaguered spirit as well as a source of hot water for my taps! There is something very companionable about an open coal fire.

No light, no television, no vacuum cleaner. With all my dogs, daily hoovering was a must, but now I was reduced to brush and dustpan.

What a relief to have my rather dark cottage illuminated by the sun, and how soon that went down and it was back to the candles. I was rather extravagant with those in the first two days, but when I realised that it might be many days before the power was restored I began to ration them.

Early on Saturday morning, I decided that I must get the PVC sheeting needed for the conservatory roof. I knew by then that it was up to me. Everyone else was too busy on emergency work to worry about a mere conservatory, but to me it was essential, so out I went.

I didn't try my usual route to Tonbridge as this narrow wooded lane was certainly to be blocked, I thought. I discovered afterwards that this was a mistake. Tina's boy friend Philip had gone that way to work the previous day, and on encountering a fallen tree had simply got out of his car with his chainsaw and cleared it.

I tried to go through the village and past the big house of Fairlawne. No hope, all roads closed at that end. I turned and tried another lane and emerged triumphant on the Fairlawne road only to be stopped at the next village, Shipbourne. I did drive for some way past the Road Closed signs only to see that the problem was indeed a big one – a number of huge oaks lying shattered on the road.

Returning to Shipbourne, I tried the back way through Hildenborough Road and Riding Wood, full of bluebells in Spring but now a scene of desolation. It seemed most unlikely that this would be a through road but to my relief the debris had been pulled aside to give passage for a single car, a zigzag path indeed but possible to take at a walking pace.

I think it was here that I first realised the vastness of the damage which had been done in those few wild hours. It was like the end of the world, somehow made worse by the fresh greenness of those shattered trunks and branches, so alive in their death, entangled with black festoons of electric cables and all shining and gleaming with rainwater still running over their leaves.

And silence, not a bird, and a bone-chilling cold and the realisation that things would never look the same – this damage was too great to repair.

Having gained Hildenborough, however, I found the DIY store and was in time to buy four of their last six PVC sheets. Returning to the village I saw Robin the builder and told him to forget about my conservatory as I was now able to repair the roof myself.

He said he still had six houses to do but would fix my drainpipe when he could. I waited a long while. I spent the rest of that Saturday mending the roof and felt so much relief when it was once more whole.

My new greenhouse – bought and erected, with much swearing by me at incomprehensible instructions, only a few weeks before the calamity – was miraculously unhurt, not a pane cracked.

A new sound was heard in the land – the whine of the chainsaws – and the air was full of woodsmoke. Some of the giant oaks which had been torn right out of the ground had root balls the size of houses. When these were fired on site they burned for days, huge leering red ovens throwing a sinister glow across the fields.

It was a week before the Shipbourne road was cleared but, considering the vastness of the problem, the gangs worked miracles. It took longer for the electricity to flow again and even longer for the telephones to work, but all these services must have been in a flurry of frantic effort. Millions of trees had been destroyed, many houses and other buildings badly damaged and some lives also lost. Taken all in all, we came off very lightly in my little house.

A few days after the storm, Dot invited me to dinner. Although there was still no power, she said they were having a hot meal of chicken. Nobby had bought a big tray of chicken joints from the supermarket and proposed to cook them under the living room fire. This was a great success but remains memorable to me for a remarkable coup by Peanut, Tina's old Dandie Dinmont.

Everyone was too busy to take any notice of Peanut, but the smell of cooking chicken was obviously more than she could stand, and, making a sudden raid from her post among the legs and feet of the assembled company, she grabbed a chicken joint, and before anyone could stop her, swallowed it whole.

We waited apprehensively for repercussions of one sort or another, but there never were any. Peanut got it down, kept it down and, as far as anyone could see, digested it without any trouble, thank you very much!

The hurricane inspired great deeds in many people and this was one of them!

When I had found myself in Hildenborough looking for PVC, I called on my friend Bobbie who lived there. This was the same friend who had come to Storm's thirteenth birthday party. All was well with her and her phone still worked. I asked if I might phone Clarisse to let her know I was all right.

I did not have her father's number with me, and directory enquiries refused to divulge it as it was ex-directory. However the operator admitted the exceptional circumstances and offered to ask them if they would accept a call from me. This they did and Clarisse was more than relieved to hear my voice for the storm had been equally violent where she was.

She returned a few days later and we took a drive around the neighbourhood to view the damage. Every approach road had been blocked and was only navigable through a narrow trail between ruined giants.

A little church sat in a vast amphitheatre of broken and battered branches, while lower down the same lane a majestic curving avenue of beeches lay like a row of dominoes toppled by a contemptuous blow. Here and there a stand of trees had been snapped at about fifteen feet from the ground and stood like bad and broken teeth, perhaps the hardest of all the storm's obscenities to see.

There were no autumn tints for us that year. Because the rain had been very heavy and prolonged, all the trees had been wearing full heads of rich green foliage. Because of the rain too, the ground was saturated so that they were standing in what was not much more than thin soup. It was these two factors taken together which allowed the tempest to wreak so much damage and take our beautiful old trees right out of their anchorages.

Afterwards the leaves hung black and shrivelled from the sombre skeletons of the ruined boughs. Skylines had changed, woods had been felled, paths obliterated, and talk of replanting had a hollow ring. Our lovely lanes were disfigured by the raw ends of sawn trunks. Chainsaws droned endlessly and bonfires smoked.

I know that in other parts of the world, such events are common, but we are just not used to them. We had lost many trees that were hundreds of years old, some woodlands normally open to the public were not safe to walk in for over a year, and many houses were badly damaged. I was so lucky that my little house escaped serious harm.

Tucked into the hillside, it must have seen many storms, but I'm sure that it never weathered a worse one than the October storm of 1987.

No one who lived through it will forget it, and I am not the only one whom it has left permanently nervous of anything like a strong wind.

Only two years later we had a similar storm, but this one happened during daylight hours and of course most of the trees at risk had already gone. I had picked up a Welsh terrier from the village for a trim and became very uneasy working in my conservatory as the winds strengthened. Also I knew the electricity would soon fail, so I clipped furiously.

I decided eventually to run her home during a slight lull. I delivered her with relief, seized my money somewhat impolitely and, mumbling something about ringing for her next appointment, fled.

By the time I got home, the roof of the conservatory had gone again. The wind was gusting up to a hundred miles an hour. This time I had better luck. Although I spent an uncomfortable twenty minutes perched on a chair holding the roof down until help arrived from the farm to secure it with paving slabs, a customer of mine, who had a small building firm, obligingly brought some men over and completely replaced it.

They did a good job, although I think they considered me a bit over-fussy in insisting that the new PVC sheets be laid so that the prevailing wind went over the joins instead of getting into them like a crowbar and taking the lot off again.

This second great wind was thankfully succeeded by a long period of calm and, at the present date, we have had no more storms to compare with either of them.

Long may it continue. The only Storm I wish to remember is the one who, despite her name, threw the gold and warmth of her own blessed sunshine over thirteen happy years.

23

Big Break

Agatha Christie, at the start of her autobiography, said that she would not be able to relate her life in strict chronological order but instead could only dip her hand into the pool of her memories and see what came up. I can sympathise with this as it seems difficult to the point of impossibility to remember even the order in which events happened, and even harder to be able to give them their correct dates.

The only reliable record which I possess is my breeding register, kept in a tatty old exercise book. My daughter Naomi kindly bound this for me in a handsome dark red, and this has preserved it.

Unfortunately she got some of the pages out of order and, although I have carefully recorded the names of stud dogs used, I regret that I didn't always enter the pedigrees of the litters for future reference. This information is around somewhere among my other papers but not easy to retrieve.

Black mark.

The hurricane, however, did its best to blow us to bits in October 1987 and is a date not easy to forget. Two months later Clarisse and I spent what we afterwards called our 'Christmas at the vets'. This began a day or two before the festivities, and, although I can't now recall exactly what all our emergencies were, they really were all situations which we could not ignore. How lucky we were, the surgery was always open, the vets always dedicated and kind, the nurses always sweet, competent and sympathetic.

One thing I am sure of was that I was in and out several times with Shari, then pregnant with her fifth and last litter. Things were not going well and on Christmas Eve the vet decided on a Caesarean. Two vets attended her, ably assisted by the head nurse, while Clarisse and I, in an adjoining room, did our best to stimulate the pathetic puppies as they were born, tired and weakened by their struggle to emerge into the light of day. With vigorous rubbing with rough towels and a certain amount of mouth to mouth resuscitation we had some success but three of the weakest puppies had to be left behind in the incubator, and all these three pups died in the night.

I took the remainder up into my bedroom when we got home and tried to settle Shari with her family in the big box there. Usually the day after the birth of a litter is a very peaceful one, with the bitch tired and content to sleep with her babies. But this time Shari was very restless and unhappy.

I had asked for her to be spayed during the proceedings. Feeding the puppies never seems to present a problem to a bitch after a Caesarean and Shari was not licking her wound or worrying her stitches, but she seemed quite unable to settle down, and this is dangerous for newborn puppies even when they have not had such a rocky start as this bunch had.

I was up all night with her while Clarisse coped with everything else, so on Christmas Day we were back at the surgery.

The vet diagnosed an infection, gave her a jab and some tablets and, to my relief, she went home far happier and settled down at once to look after her family with her customary skill and tenderness.

But our troubles were by no means over for on my return I had found Samba on three legs and apparently in great pain. Whatever could she have done? So, leaving Clarisse in charge, it was back to the vet.

By the time we arrived, Samba was putting her foot down gingerly and he could find nothing wrong. Home again armed with painkillers. Fortunately this contretemps cleared up with no other treatment than rest. I can only think she must have caught and wrenched it somehow. Probably just wanted her share of the limelight.

Collapsing on to my bed, I prepared to sleep with one eye open. Shari had produced ten puppies, five boys and five girls, and of these five had died, one boy and four girls. Most of my enquiries at that time were for bitches, naturally. Now I have never had trouble sleeping and by then I was so exhausted that I went out like a light. Fortunately Shari did the same and all the family were safe and feeding well when I awoke, but on going downstairs I was greeted with more bad news. Clarisse had been up all night with Spice the Dandie who was having difficulty breathing.

Only one thing to do – you've guessed. Back to the vets. A week or two previously, Spice had been X-rayed and the results of other tests had come through. It was cancer of the lungs. Nothing could be done for her, my dear little dog who was much loved at the vets as well as by me, and I don't think there was a dry eye in the place when she was quietly given peace. She was thirteen years old.

What a Christmas! It tailed off gradually and I was presented with a bill of nearly a thousand pounds. This was an even bigger amount in those days than it is now, and how good it was to have a firm of vets who were so kind and considerate. I paid a few hundreds, all I had at the time, and thereafter at least fifty a month, and more if I had it, until it was all paid off.

Never once did they even remind me of this debt and I continued to take my dogs to them whenever they needed it. Today the whole atmosphere has changed. Vets are big business with the accent heavily on business. Prices are so high as to make it practically impossible for poor people to take their animals in unless they can go to any of the excellent free services available in some districts.

Soon after this hilarious Christmas, Clarisse went back to her father and began taking a degree course as a mature student. She enjoyed this very much but was saddened by the impossibility of keeping her old pointer with her. This meant that she often came back to see us as Clover continued to live with me.

It was on one of these visits that she went to see a friend who lived nearby and on going back to her car caught her foot in a pothole on the drive and broke her leg. It was such a small hole it seemed impossible that it could have caused so much damage, but, when I went to the scene and experimentally put my own heel into the hole, I was surprised to find how strongly it gripped my foot. Her friend drove her back here so that she could leave Clover before taking her to Casualty.

Casualty wanted to send her home and even advised her that the best thing to do was to walk on it, but Clarisse is not a doctor's daughter for nothing and flatly refused to go. At last they got a more clued-up medico to see her and he promptly had her put to bed. It was a very bad Potts fracture, one of the worst types of break, necessitating an operation and several weeks in hospital.

Poor Clarisse was very down as, apart from all the pain, it meant giving up her university place and, having now no home of her own, she did not know where to go or what to do on coming out.

To me there was only one answer to these problems. I dismantled my spare bed, slid the bits down the stairs, and put them together again in the front room which I converted into a bedroom for her.

There was only one drawback to this plan. Although there were no puppies using it as a nursery at that time and although its permanent tenants, my books, raised no objection to her presence, this was the room above all others favoured by gangs of marauding spiders.

Enthusiasm for dogs and the fine arts are not the only things which Clarisse and I have in common. We are both also rampant arachnophobes.

Frankly, I could not have slept there. Not only is Clarisse made of sterner stuff, but the pain of her leg and the difficulty of coping with a massive plaster made her realise that this little room was ideal. Just inside the front door and on a level with all other essential offices, it was a haven worth braving monsters for. But she had some bad moments there.

One day just after she had struggled in and sat on the bed I heard piercing shrieks and screams coupled with agonised cries of 'Dora! Dora! Why don't you come!' I don't think to this day that she has quite forgiven me for not rushing in at once, but the fact was that I knew from the sound of her voice what was the matter.

First I dashed to the conservatory for my trusty cylinder vacuum cleaner and hauled it with me to the rescue.

Earlier in the day, she had put a letter from her daughter down on her pillow, and now, on sitting down and picking it up, had found an enormous black spider on it.

No matter how she turned the paper, this animal kept crawling towards her. She was afraid to throw the whole thing away in case it disappeared under the bed and made sleep impossible for the foreseeable future.

Once I appeared with the cleaner already plugged in, I was able to remove the invader bodily. I am sorry if this offends any lovers of the crawling classes, but it is this ploy which has made it possible for me to live alone in my house.

The plain fact is that we can't both be in it, and, as I have to pay the bills, I feel I have priority. These animals should keep out.

Later on, I took advantage of a council scheme for repairing old properties and was able to replace the old front door with a much better fitting one. This has since been completely sealed against draughts, and the result is that large spiders hardly ever gain admittance now, to my great relief, but Clarisse still talks about that awful day and the fact that I did not immediately come galloping to her rescue.

As soon as she was able to manage the stairs, we moved the bed back up into the little spare room. This became her own refuge and she redecorated it herself, putting up a very pretty paper, sporting demure stripes of tiny pink rosebuds on a ivory background.

I bought a flatpack dressing table for the knock-down price of thirty pounds, white with pink handles. This was duly installed, but somehow there was never enough room for all the belongings which she had managed to salvage from the marital home. Dainty and fresh as it now looked, the room could never quite digest the bundles and parcels of stuff which to be honest were not only hers but clutter of my own which we could not quite eject from its former home. I had always made my own clothes and had stockpiled a many-coloured store of materials mostly bought in the market, and where else could it all go? Even now, I still mine this seam when I need new trousers or a matching top.

Nursing Clarisse was not the easiest job in the world as, to a naturally lively and active person, it was very hard to bear this new life of unavoidable restriction of movement. Luckily we had a lot to talk about, and to my surprise I found that television, that blessing of the lonely, was largely an undiscovered country to her.

This was because she had been allowed very little say as to what was watched in her former home and simply did not know what good things were available among the documentary and educational programmes.

I am an early riser and, at that time, the Open University slot on Channel Two often gave delectable fare in the Arts and I seldom missed them. Renaissance painting and architecture and sixteenth century history are among her favourite things so we never missed anything shown on these subjects. A lot of comedy programmes too we found were to our mutual taste.

The dogs were good and careful around her, and her beloved Clover, so gentle and so loving, kept her velvety brown head always within fondling distance. But Clarisse was always in great pain and for some weeks unable to move even about the room without difficulty.

One lovely day, I felt that Clarisse deserved as much change of view as my premises could provide, and thought it would be a good idea to take her to the end of the garden. Once through the screen of the willow's trailing tresses and turned to look towards the house, one seems to be in another world. It's a world of many greens: emerald, gold, sage-grey and conifer-dark; a world of shifting sunlight and shadow, a quiet world of birdsong and sweet breezes. That's what I thought.

Unfortunately my patient had developed a natural and great fear of falling and causing further damage to her perpetually painful leg, so I eased her through the back door and into the hospital wheelchair without giving her any warning of my benign purpose. I had reckoned that with a bit of a rush to start with, I would be able to push her right up the slope to the designated position for her treat.

Unfortunately the garden path is not really wide enough for a wheelchair and our way was bumpy. My helpless passenger was convinced that she would be upset before we stopped and gave tongue in no uncertain manner. Dark woods and golden meadows, orchards and hills, rang to her screams of rage and terror. No, I didn't upset her and, once installed in the preordained spot with a book and a drawing pad, I think she saw my point.

No doubt her pleasure was severely curtailed by the fear of the return journey. Being downhill this was a good bit easier for both of us. I can't say that Clarisse ever expressed gratitude for my thoughtfulness in this instance, and it was never repeated.

It was bad enough for the poor woman when I took her out in my mini, this not being the most comfortable of cars for an invalid, but necessary until the plaster came off and she could drive herself again.

But on that happy day, we found to our consternation that her leg had been set so that her heel came nowhere down to the ground. It took a lot of physiotherapy and hard swearing until we managed to make that work properly again.

As soon as she was mobile again, Clarisse began looking for work that she could do to support herself and her dog. To her delight, she obtained a post as guide at Leeds Castle which has been described as the most beautiful castle in the world.

I drove her over there for her interview and frankly did not think it would be possible for her to do the job. For a start it is nearly twenty miles away and I could not have taken her to work and picked her up again at the end of the day. Driving was still painful for her and on top of that Leeds covers a great deal of ground. To take parties round it involves so much walking and climbing of stairs that it seemed impossible. Even the guides' car park was a long walk from the building.

But Clarisse was nothing if not determined. She had fallen deeply in love with these low grey walls set among their silver lakes and moats, and gloried in being able to serve them with her knowledge of her favourite period. The pageantry of its history, the splendour of its grounds, luminous with daffodils and flowering trees in Spring, echoing with the cries of its peacocks and waterbirds, so inspired her with enthusiasm that somehow she overcame all obstacles.

Not only did she become a first class guide but had her reward for her stoic refusal to give in to pain in that all this forced exercise did in the end help to heal her leg – in so far as it ever was healed, for the sad fact is that it has never been really right since that unlucky day.

24
Blossom

And what was happening to my cottage all this time? As an edifice of venerable years, it did qualify for some very opportune grants so that, in addition to the new door, I was at various times able to have new windows too – copying as far as possible their old small-paned cottage style – and to have the gable ends repointed.

This last was really necessary as up in the loft you could see daylight through the walls. Robin the builder did this for me and in fact the whole house. Besides all this, he always looked after my slate roof, and a few years ago also painted the exterior.

In fact, he has always been a tower of strength as well as being ready with advice when needed. Luckily the repointing took place before the hurricane – or the whole place might have been blown away!

Robin was only one of several good men who have helped me from the day I moved in, beginning with my dear bank manager, Dickie Bird, including Phil the garage man who kept my old minivans running, and never forgetting Messrs Oliver and Noble, my two vets, always so kind and understanding. Some of these are no longer with us but I remember them all with gratitude.

Even the most obstinately self-sufficient of us need help now and then. There was the day when an egg box, carelessly thrown on the fire, went up the chimney and set it on fire. This should not have been a big issue. After all, chimneys are built to contain fires. But after a call to the fire brigade had produced not one but two fire engines, half an hour's work with floods of water had still not quenched the blaze because the men were unable to locate the centre of the fire. Then a fireman traipsing up the stairs luckily saw smoke issuing from the blocked-up hearth in my bedroom. They discovered that the chimney stack in the loft, which joined the flues from two fireplaces, had a hole in it. The burning egg box had floated up as far as this, gone through into the other chimney, and come to rest in the old bedroom grate behind its hardboard cover. With this discovery, they were able to extinguish it but it took a long time and I was left feeling sooty, very substandard and upset.

I remembered an old customer, a builder, who lived some way away and rang him up and explained my plight. In next to no time he arrived, bringing his little wife with him who plied me with coffee while her husband inspected the damage. Not to worry, he said, he would fix it, and sure enough next day he came back, went aloft and bricked up the hole, making my chimney once again safe and usable. He also took time to enlarge the trap into the roof space which had probably been designed either for midgets or juvenile chimney sweeps.

Thank you, Horace, another angel in an unlikely guise.

After Dot and Nobby had left their cottage, it and the adjoining one were knocked together and given to Roger the farm manager. I hope I haven't bothered Roger too much over the years we have been neighbours, but whenever I have asked him for assistance it has always been given generously and promptly – whether in helping to stop my conservatory roof being blown away or in the little matter of Blossom.

After the much lamented death of her beloved Clover, Clarisse thought that she would give a home to another gundog. We heard that one was down on its luck in an animal shelter and decided to go and look it over. We were told that it had been running wild for two weeks before the police had managed to trap it and take it to the refuge, and had been seen pulling up grass and eating the roots, also the bark of trees. They had wormed and inoculated it and given it good food but it was still very distressed.

Neither of us will ever forget our first sight of Blossom as the kennelman brought her round the corner of the kennel building. She looked like a cross between a giraffe and a windmill with legs flailing in all directions. Rich brown roan coat, long ears and mournful eyes: Clarisse's soft heart was touched and we put the dog into the back of her car and brought her home.

She was driving by now so it was I who sat in the back with her new prize and tried to reassure the dog as we went. Clarisse by this time had finalised her divorce and bought her own house. This was just as well as for the next five nights Blossom gave her no sleep, wandering restlessly round the stairs and rooms moaning.

As Clarisse was working, I had the dog during the day. Luckily again my mob raised no objection. Getting used to two homes at once after having none could not have been easy for this poor creature but at last she did begin to settle down and become easier in her mind. And grow.

We had been told that she was probably eighteen months old but it soon became evident that not only was she barely half that age but that she was certainly not the wire-haired pointer we had been offered but an Italian Spinone, a much bigger breed.

This was a big puzzle, for Spinone puppies at that time were fetching very hefty prices, and it was evident that she had been well bred. So why had no one ever enquired about her?

We did eventually find what might well have been the answer, and a very hard-hearted one we thought it. Meanwhile, Clarisse found herself with a very presentable member of a breed she had long had a yen for but never expected to be able to afford.

She worked hard on her new acquisition and it is much to her credit that Blossom eventually did settle down and become a great dog.

She was Clarisse's, heart and soul, from the first day. One might have expected her to think I was her rescuer since it was I who had sat with her in the back of the car reassuring and stroking her on her first journey home, but not so. She knew without any shadow of a doubt that she belonged to Clarisse and nobody else.

Inexcusably I have omitted all mention of Heather. When Tina left me in search of more money and wider fields, I advertised for another helper. I did this by putting up a carefully worded card in the vets, and after a gap of some weeks Heather applied for the job.

This ranks high among the good things that have come to me in life, for Heather is one of the nicest people I have ever met. Besides being utterly reliable and unfailingly helpful, she is a completely besotted animal lover, and all the dogs, residents and customers alike, adore her.

So it was Heather who, coming in one afternoon after her lunch, informed me that Blossom was on the conservatory roof. Frankly I didn't believe her – it was obviously nonsense. Only actual inspection proved that it was in fact true.

Blossom, by then a fully grown and well-nourished Spinone weighing perhaps a hundred pounds, was calmly taking the air while strolling round on my PVC roof. It was high summer and my bedroom window was open. She must have slipped upstairs and jumped out of the open window onto the slate roof some five feet below.

Inspection, in fact, showed some disturbance of the slates where she had landed. Then she had walked down on to the PVC and now she was stuck and looked only too likely to take the quick way down through the plastic.

Heather climbed on to a garden chair and I passed a lead up to her so that she could slip it through the collar and keep Blossom in one place while I sought help. She was much too heavy for us to lift her down and, if she had jumped or fallen, she could hardly have avoided injury.

Desperately I rang the farm and was more than thankful to get straight through to Roger, to whom I described our emergency and begged for help. True to form, he acted at once and in less than five minutes he arrived, bringing with him two stalwart assistants.

We pushed the garden table right up to the wall and the two men climbed on to it. One of them managed to get a firm hold of the marooned Blossom and handed her down to the other, who passed her to Roger on the ground. I felt it only right to assure them throughout that she didn't bite, and it was obvious to me at any rate that she wouldn't. It did occur to me afterwards how much this poor dog had changed since Clarisse had adopted her, because in the frankly loopy state with which she reacted to any unexpected situation or incident for some time after her first arrival, anything could have happened.

One positive result of this adventure was that the roof had held up under a completely un-looked for test, and it is still as good as ever. But we never risked Blossom going walkabout up there again.

Blossom always had very sore eyes with drooping inflamed lids, and whatever Clarisse did they never got any better. She went from vet to vet in a desperate search for a cure and was eventually told by a specialist that her dog was a sufferer from 'cherry eye'. A large red ball can be seen in the inner corner of the eye, and apparently both had been affected. This obviously would have ruined any chance of success in the show ring and would also have made any puppies she might have had unsaleable.

Her owners, whoever they were, must have taken her to a vet for treatment. It is likely that he or she was not a very good practitioner, for instead of doing the best – and no doubt difficult – procedure of stitching the red ball down underneath the third eyelid, the whole thing had been cut out instead.

Clarisse's specialist was fiercely angry about this as the third eyelid produces about a third of the eye's tears, and without it she was bound to suffer from dry eye. This was made worse as she also had out-turned eyelids (ectropion).

Had she escaped and been left to her fate or had she been deliberately thrown out? We'll never know, but surely her previous owners would have looked for their lost dog if she had not had this problem.

It was a tragedy. More and more remedies were tried without success until Clarisse was putting either drops or cream into her eyes six times a day. This was trying enough in itself but what was worse was to see no improvement but a steady deterioration in the condition.

After struggling with this problem for six years and being told that nothing could be done to alleviate Blossom's increasing pain, my friend felt that she could no longer prolong her sufferings. Poor Blossom, fate certainly dealt her a bad hand, made worse by the heartlessness of her early human contacts.

Quite apart from all these medical considerations, she had undoubtedly been harshly treated. She had odd wild panics, sparked off by hearing a loud voice or even by seeing a plate handed from one person to another – probably she had been the target of flying crockery during her puppyhood. I believe too that she may have been kept shut in an outside loo as she certainly thought a toilet was something to drink out of. As she soon gave up that particular practice when living in civilised society, it seems as if it must have been a habit forced upon her by necessity.

At least she had some years of real happiness with Clarisse whom she adored with her whole heart, and during those years she never again experienced hunger or harsh treatment. She had a happy friendship with my dogs, plenty of exercise and every luxury that her Mum could supply.

I think Clarisse will always feel some guilt at ending her life while she was still in her prime, gentle and loving. To my mind, there is no doubt that this was the only merciful and right decision, when we remember her red and suppurating eyes and the agony she must have endured. But it is always hard.

25

Paradise Threatened

My cottage was chosen for strictly pragmatic reasons, as I have explained, but it became increasingly apparent that I had struck very lucky. The first clue came when an architect customer of mine, on enquiring what I had paid for it, exclaimed 'The land alone is worth that!'

I looked around my domain and wondered. The ground slopes, and a large part of it is heavily shaded by woodland. It is on a spring line, so parts of the garden are always soggy – but others are remarkably dry and crumbly.

Not the easiest plot to manage, but certainly one full of character!

It also has almost magical properties for gardening. If a plant likes it here, it likes it a lot and will rapidly grow to alarming proportions.

As some gave up early on and others flourished, my early planning was soon out of date. Nettles can be ten feet tall, elderberry seedlings and brambles seem to take over during a weekend, and, when the huge willow was eventually cut down, its annual rings proved to be an inch wide.

The countryside roundabout is an area bounded by three large towns, motorways and railways. It is a delightful rural pocket that has escaped the London coast-to-coast development of most of Kent. Roland Hilder has made it famous with his many beautiful paintings of hop-gardens, oast houses and farmland.

When I arrived, I was astonished to discover villagers speaking a country dialect in a Kentish accent. They even understood the name of my cottage, as 'caterways' is an old Kentish word meaning diagonally set.

'Tain't caterways at all', protested Tom when I put up the name board, and I had to explain that it was the name of my old house where my dog breeding had begun in earnest, and that I had kept it as my kennel name ever since.

The views of the surrounding countryside from the garden or the cottage windows are a constant pleasure, marred only by the electricity and telephone cables that blight so much of Kent. Without moving from home, I can see woods, fields and hedges, a duck pond, a beautiful oast house, a Georgian manor house and, best of all, can glimpse the twelfth century manor of the local Monument.

I can count on the fingers of one hand the dwellings in this little hamlet, and it is so peaceful that wildlife is often seen. My bird table encourages the small tits and finches, while doves, magpies and woodpeckers are common in the wood. Many game birds are raised on neighbouring estates and I must say pheasants seem the most bird-brained of the lot. One of their favourite occupations is walking in the roads attempting to get run over.

Living so close to nature is a mixed blessing and I have had to take a firm line with rats, mice, moles and rabbits. The local badgers dig such deep holes in the banks that they often cover the lane in slippery clay. And then there are the foxes.

To tell the truth, I am not very pro-fox. For every handsome red-jacketed hero flashing a bushy tail with a white tip, there are dozens of dingy, scrawny specimens flipping weightlessly up banks and into hedges as one's car approaches. Foxes are cruel. Given the chance, they will kill mercilessly and for fun, and they shed diseases such as mange and hepatitis which infect our domestic animals.

If rabies comes to this country, there will no doubt be terrible, hysterical slaughter of foxes and other wildlife. Surely it would be more humane and sensible to work for a steady reduction in numbers now.

Hunting is claimed to be less cruel than other methods of disposal, but how can we be sure? All methods are grim, and the large scale destruction of packs of hounds troubling to contemplate, whether it is a routine cull at the end of the season or the projected ending of legal blood sports.

One aspect of hunting that does stick in my throat is the element of parade, the dandified overdone spit and polish of horse and rider out to kill for pleasure.

A few years ago, I was driving into market with my friend Dot. A Kentish countrywoman to her bones, Dot has a deep-felt contempt and distrust of 'toffs'.

Chatting in my scruffy mini, we saw members of the hunt approaching, so I kept pulling into the hedge to let them pass in the narrow lane. Riders hacking around the countryside usually smile, nod or lift a hand in thanks for this courtesy. But the members of this cavalcade, who were mostly the same riders on the same horses, went by as if in a trance without acknowledging us by so much as the flicker of an eyelid. I thought of Oscar Wilde's 'the unspeakable in pursuit of the uneatable'. Dot muttered a stream of invective.

Eyes front, heels down, they stalked onward, every bit of kit winking and gleaming, manes plaited, hooves varnished. Surely this was more appropriate for a horse show? In the muddy lane it seemed somehow obscene.

The last riders passed. We drew out of the hedge and drove cautiously round the next bend only to shout with laughter. Jogging quietly down the middle of the lane well behind the hunt was the fox.

There was much excitement in Plaxtol when a television company chose it for an educational programme of the evolution of a typical English village. A Roman villa stood nearby and there are traces of Roman vineyards. The village has been in continuous occupation ever since, and no doubt before.

It has the distinction of an unusual church built during Cromwell's Commonwealth, when destroying church property was more the norm. Evidence of hop farming, papermaking, medieval life and much else survives. I realised even my own short muddy lane is rich in history for those who have eyes to see.

No wonder I always feel such deep pleasure whenever returning to my home. No wonder I was so alarmed when one of the projected routes for the Channel Tunnel Rail Link threatened to destroy the peace of the Bourne valley. The map was unbelievable. Route Three came south-east to a point a mile from my cottage, then changed direction abruptly and made for Folkestone and the Channel.

The Plaxtol Action Group was formed and soon had organised a trip to Westminster to protest. One hundred and fifteen of us travelled in two coaches to join five thousand protesters from villages all over Kent. We had pictures painted by local schoolchildren to hold up at the windows whenever we spotted TV cameras.

On arrival, we queued up to get into a hall to meet our local MPs who stoutly asserted their devotion to our cause but had no time to listen to our spokesmen. However, we had at least added to the numbers making the pilgrimage, and in the end the village was spared when another more direct route was chosen. Since then the lane and everything I can see from the cottage has been designated a Conservation Area, so is protected to some extent from future planning disasters.

When my father moved out of London in the thirties, he luxuriated in his Kentish bungalow and called it 'my little bit of heaven'. That house is now enveloped in an expanding London and I moved further out to find my own rural haven. So far it may have occasionally been Paradise Threatened, but never Paradise Lost.

Changes

Before the Romans, long before, a folk
From Neolithic times roamed where my cottage stands.
With little skill for farming, did they hunt
Across my garden, searching wood and stream
In desperation for their winter food?
Their lives were short and brutish, did they smile
To hear my larks and blackbirds sing for joy
Or laugh to see the hares box in the Spring
Or watch the kestrel dropping from the sky?

To think that Vikings raided where I stand,
And Saxon churls in terror drove their pigs
To hide them in the limestone clefts o'ergrown
With couch and bramble in the hilly wood.
The lord who built the manor dwelt at ease,
His villeins kept him fed, and, huddled, slept
Among the rushes on his great hall's floor.
How many children cried in chill and want
While he in silks and furs fawned on his king?

This stretch of meadow is my garden now,
The hunted are the mouse and rat and mole.
The hunting dogs are mine, my gentle friends.
But as the seedling ash that I weed out
Among my flowerbeds is the certain heir
Of England's mighty forests, so the blood
Of these my forebears must run in my veins,
Making me mourn their sorrows, shun their fears,
Cramped in a lifespan half the length of mine.
This cottage, built to house a labouring man,
With wife and children, seven, eight or ten,
My kingdom now, with comfort and with ease
That Roman, Saxon, Viking never knew,
Cossets me with the wonders of the age.
The round world's art and music, wisdom, news,
Flicker and sing, a shining in my room.

My car stands at my door, my garden flowers,
My dogs sleep in its shade, while all around
The ancient hills, the woods, the gleaming sky
Look on me with amaze, as who should say
'What have you done to merit this? Why you?'

Epilogue

My mother died in September 2001 after a six-day illness at the end of her eighty-first year. While in hospital she directed me to the manuscript of her second book. It lay in a thick file beside her faithful Amstrad in the middle of the sitting room table, where she had worked on it so hard during her last year. There were 26 completed chapters, and on disk various poems and sketches she had written over the years, all of which have helped to make this book.

When she came to live in the hamlet of Old Soar outside Plaxtol village, her family were concerned. She depended utterly on her minivan and seemed very short of neighbours. There was no gas, no mains water or drainage and no public transport. The lane was steep and often flooded. How could she hope to manage, with or without dogs, as she grew older?

Well, she has had the last laugh, I am glad to say. At no time was she crippled, or confused, or too frail to climb the stairs. She drove her car to the end, saw neighbours come and go with equanimity, and although planning to move on to a smaller breed, never had to give up her beloved Airedales. She put her affairs in order two months before she died, and chose to take a Terry Pratchett paperback into hospital.

Her funeral was held on a sunny day in the Cromwellian village church and was attended by dozens of fellow terrier enthusiasts, Christina's clan, family, friends and customers, and her vet, now retired. And I am sure she noticed one young Airedale there, too.

There are surprising omissions in this account of her thirty happy years in Caterways Cottage. Her friends and acquaintances made up an astonishing spectrum of travellers, millionaires, professionals of every stripe, craftsmen and labourers. A farmer, a Japanese policeman, the owner of a national business, a bookbinder, a magician and a plumber are just some of the people who sought her out for her professional expertise or advice.

It was a great excitement for her when her first book of memoirs, 'Honorary Dog', was published. It went into paperback and onto Woman's Hour and she was much interviewed. It generated a steady trickle of fan mail over the years from many countries. The letters, always interesting, were carefully preserved. Following this triumph, for several years she ran a creative writing group in Tonbridge.

Towards the end of her life, there were three major health scares, but the attentions of the NHS provided her with a pacemaker and a new knee, turning the clock back for her.

She liked to participate in the wider world of dogs, visiting Crufts and Windsor shows, joining canine campaigns and writing for specialist magazines. Her own showing and breeding career was prematurely curtailed, but a new enthusiasm was attending Airedale Fun Days.

In moments of insight, she knew that her best role in life was as a friend. Although cursory in her everyday attention to mere human beings, she had the rare quality of coming through with magnificent, uncritical support when people were really down on their luck. She could be fearless, energetic and inventive in their cause, for her sharp wits made her a force to be reckoned with.

However, the love of her life was dogs, more specifically Airedales, and had been from a girl. As she said, 'They have given me more joy in life than anything else.'

Many people dream of retreating to a cottage with roses round the door, of living in the country with beloved animals. Many people visited to see the reality. For my mother, born and bred in smoky Southwark, had made the dream come true.

Naomi